ESCAPING

THE TIGER'S

CLAWS

HARAMBEEPRESS

ESCAPING

THE TIGER'S

CLAWS

A Journey of Faith
Three Years, Eight Months, and Twenty Days

Pastor Chamron Phal's story
as told to Susan Bailey Burke

ESCAPING THE TIGER'S CLAWS FROM SUSAN BAILEY BURKE
Harambee Press is an imprint of LPCBooks
a division of Iron Stream Media
100 Missionary Ridge, Birmingham, AL 35242

ISBN: 978-1-64526-265-7
Copyright © 2020 by Susan Bailey Burke
Cover design by Hannah Linder
Interior design by AtriTex Technologies Pvt Ltd.

Available in print from your local bookstore, online, or from the publisher at: ShopLPC.com

This is a true story of the life of Pastor Chamron Phal as told to Susan Bailey Burke.

Brought to you by the creative team at LPCBooks: Edwina Perkins, Jessica Everson

Library of Congress Cataloging-in-Publication Data
Bailey Burke, Susan
Escaping the Tiger's Claws/Susan Bailey Burke 1st ed.

Printed in the United States of America

ACKNOWLEDGMENTS

I WANT TO THANK PASTOR Chamron Phal for meeting with me every Wednesday for five years and having the courage to share his difficult journey in the Cambodian Killing Fields to make this book a reality. As we worked, I felt the presence of the Holy Spirit.

I am thankful for my long-time friend Todd Kerns, who connected me with Edwina Perkins, managing editor of Harambee Press with the publishing house Iron Steam Media. Jessica R. Everson, my general editor, worked closely with me for a year, editing my manuscript. Authors Kay Strom and Dan Kline invested time with me over five years at the Mount Hermon Christian Writers Conference. I appreciate how they mentored me, a first-time author.

I want to thank Dawn Lindholm, who graciously hosted me at her home in Mount Hermon during the conferences, and my best friend Janice Hansson, who met with me weekly and read the manuscript. Spending time in Cambodia with Pastor Chamron gave Janice insights into the horror of the Killing Fields and compassion for its people. My weekly Bible study group supported me and listened to my updates on the book's progress.

I thank my church family for their faith in me, especially Pastor Nancy Lewis, Tom Ayer, Joan Sweetman, and Jim and Lynda Hampton.

I could not have done this without the loving support of my husband Denny. He served coffee, tea, and encouragement to Chamron, Janice, and me during our many hours of work. He faithfully held my hand and prayed for me as I sat at the computer searching for the exact words to bring life into this story.

DEDICATION

This book is dedicated to the Cambodian people. May they experience the grace of God through Chamron's story of survival.

FOREWORD

I MET CHAMRON PHAL IN 2004. At least I think that's when it was. It may have been 2005 or 2006. My limited memory is just one of the ways in which Chamron and I differ. Mine operates in imprecise pictures and narrative that is simplified—and often amplified—over time. Chamron's is precise. He remembers dates, times, people, places, and events with a clarity I've never seen approximated in another. And he always remembers what he ate. This small, chiseled man loves food and can outeat any offensive lineman in the country.

If someone had witnessed our first encounter, they would rightly describe it as unremarkable. But during that meeting, I heard a Voice. A Voice I've heard fewer times than I have fingers on my hands. In little more than a whisper, it said, "This is your friend. Serve him." I now know this was the same Voice Chamron heard many years before in the Killing Fields.

You have a unique reading experience before you. The precision of Chamron's memory combined with Susan Burke's careful chronicling will take you on a journey through the four years, eight months, and twenty days of his Khmer Rouge nightmare. On April

17, 1975—Day One of Khmer Rouge rule—Chamron was seventeen years old, a couple of months away from his high school graduation. The odds of surviving what would befall him were minute. I'm still befuddled by his endurance.

As I write this foreword, we are all navigating through the Covid-19 pandemic. At present, around 100,000 have died in the U.S. The economy is wrecked, at least temporarily. Still, the worst of the projections have not come to pass. It is in this context that I read about my friend Chamron's battle to stay alive. Suffice it to say, I know of no one ploughing through the challenges of our day who has faced a fraction of what Chamron and millions of Cambodians endured in the latter years of the 1970s. If a flesh and blood man like Chamron could endure such suffering and go on to live a life marked by hope, grace, and generosity, what might God be able to do with you and me now?

What might we learn in the pages that follow? So much, including:

- Our normative idea of suffering is mild compared to what millions have endured through the centuries. Our myopic worldview leads us to sometimes think what is happening to us is rare or unfair. The truth is, most lives have always been, at best, difficult, and more often than not painfully and tragically hard.
- Human beings have great capacity for evil. Having listened over the years to my friend

detail the brutality he experienced, I can tell you that a choice was made in this book to hold back on the gory details and let the readers use their imaginations.

- Human beings, made in God's image as Chamron's faith and perhaps yours teaches, also have great capacity for courage, kindness, and sacrifice.
- Jesus said, "I am with you always." Biblical faith teaches there is no place or event or moment in which God leaves us alone. The radical, improbable claim of Christianity is that Jesus, when He hung on the cross, took all of history's evil on Himself. This Jesus walked and bled with Chamron throughout his terrible ordeal. His passionate proximity to all of us carries the possibility of ordinary folks like you and me becoming more resilient and hope-filled than perhaps we have anticipated.

Let Chamron Phal's life inspire you to live more courageously the life for which God has made you.

Paul V. Wilson

May 2020

AUTHOR'S NOTE

I N 2013, PASTOR CHAMRON Phal told me God had told him I was going to write the story of his survival in the Killing Fields of Cambodia.

I laughed.

"You've made a mistake," I told him. "I've never written a book. I can't even type!"

"Go home and pray about it," he said.

So I prayed.

Actually, it was more like an argument, with me listing to God all the reasons this was a crazy idea. God was silent in response. He let me argue. I imagine He was smiling.

After a few days, when I stopped arguing, I listened. Then, I heard Him speak.

Do it.

God had a plan, and I had to be obedient. So Chamron and I spent the next four years meeting every week. He told me his story, and I hand wrote every word in composition notebooks. Then, using my hunt and peck method, I typed every word.

As I stumbled along, faithfully recording page after page, event after event, God stepped in again. In 2014, He guided me to the Mount Hermon Christian

Writers Conference in Mount Hermon, California. There, I attended workshops, listened to speakers, and was trained on how to write a nonfiction book. I met wonderful writers who have encouraged me year after year.

I attended more Christian writers conferences between 2015 and 2017. I read books on different aspects of writing, and I read many nonfiction books.

Along the way, I met with Chamron every week. We prayed for him to remember details of that time forty years ago, and for me to ask the right questions to help him. We laughed, we cried, we persisted. The process seemed slow, but we both trusted God to lead the way.

Chamron knew that one day he would have this book to share when he preaches in churches and speaks at school and community groups. He gives God the glory for saving him time after time from 1975 to 1979. He promised from within the Killing Fields that if he survived, he would serve God all the days of his life. And he is keeping that promise.

It was my privilege to take this journey with Chamron. He inspires me with his faith and love for God. I hope that he will also inspire you.

~ Susan Bailey Burke

CAMBODIA

CAMBODIA IS A SOUTHEAST Asian nation that suffered genocide by the Khmer Rouge regime under the leadership of Pol Pot from 1975 to 1979. The land size is 18,100 square kilometers, comparable to the size of Missouri in the United States. The Khmer Rouge plan was to create an agrarian society free of Western influence.

The leaders forced Cambodians out of the cities to the country to be farmers. Educators, doctors, government workers, military personnel, and religious leaders were labeled enemies. Cambodians faced forced hard labor, starvation, disease, torture, and execution. Estimated deaths are between 1.7 and 3.4 million. With a large portion of the population gone, rebuilding Cambodia after the defeat of Pol Pot has been slow. Few survived the genocide, and most who did were young and mainly female. In 2015, the median age in Cambodia was 24.

From 1979 to 1991, there was no religious freedom. In 1991 Christian leaders went to the government and asked for freedom of religion to be put in the constitution. The government agreed, and now Cambodia has religious freedom. Buddhism is the official religion of

Cambodia. Today, 97 percent of Cambodians follow Buddhism, with Islam, Christianity and tribal animism making up the remainder.

TABLE OF CONTENTS

(March 1978)....................................109

Chapter 12 — Safety in Snung Village
(March 1978)....................................117

Chapter 13 — Joy Followed by Disillusionment
(January 1979)................................127

Chapter 14 — Family Reunites in French Village
(April 1979)....................................133

Chapter 15 — Selling Gold on the Thai Border
(July 1979)....................................143

Chapter 16 — Life in Thai Refugee Camps
(November 1979)............................157

Chapter 17 — New Life in a New Land
(January 1980)................................165

CHAPTER 1

....

CELEBRATION TURNED
INTO CHAOS

April 1975

"Did you hear the radio news?" Chamron called to his older brothers. "The Khmer Rouge Democratic troops have taken control of Phnom Penh. That is where Mom took Darab."

Chamron's mother had taken his sixteen-year-old sister to Cambodia's capital city, nearly 300 kilometers southeast of their home, for Darab's regular thyroid treatment. Since Chamron's father died of cancer a few years earlier, his mother and sister now made these trips alone.

The day had started as a joyous holiday for seventeen-year-old Chamron, who lived with his Grandma Rang, Grandpa Nguon, mother, and eleven siblings in Battambang City, Western Cambodia. Cambodian New Year was a special time for the family.

Grandpa Nguon had skipped his morning chores and began the celebration by playing music on the radio. Grandma Rang and Chamron's sisters were busy preparing food in the kitchen. More music, dancing, feasting, and family enjoyment should have been on the way. But what happened instead on April 17, 1975 would change Chamron's life forever.

The family had heard about the Khmer Rouge and its revolutionary efforts, which began in the jungles of eastern Cambodia, but no one had ever worried. To their knowledge, there had been no seriously alarming events during the last five years of their presence.

Compelled by the radio news and worried for their mother and sister's safety, Chamron and his brothers decided to investigate. The four boys grabbed two rusty bicycles from beside the house. Chamron held on to his older brother's waist as they bumped along the dusty path beside the rice fields.

Chamron's heart throbbed against Noe's back as they left French Village and sped two kilometers to National Road Four. They pedaled an additional five kilometers to Anlongville Village and crossed the bridge that passed through the marketplace. Leaving their bicycles, they crept onto a hill to get a better view of the road ahead.

The brothers waited and watched. One kilometer ahead, Khmer Rouge soldiers emerged from the forest and headed up the road directly toward them.

Chamron had heard about Khmer Rouge soldiers, but he had never seen them before today. Since rouge meant red, Chamron expected them to have red skin; he was surprised their skin was yellow like his. As they neared, he could see that the soldiers were dressed in black and wore sandals with rubber straps made from automobile tires. They had colorful scarves covering their necks, and vests loaded with ammunition. It frightened Chamron to see them fully armed with machine guns, AK-47s, and shoulder rockets.

"Follow me," Noe whispered, then walked into the street and toward the soldiers. Chamron and his brothers followed.

When Noe reached the first of the soldiers, he stuck an arm out and shook hands with the nearest Khmer Rouge soldier. All the brothers copied Noe as the troops passed by—shaking hands and saying "Hello! Hello! Welcome! Welcome!"

Once they'd all passed, Chamron grabbed his brother's shirt, then turned and pointed as the Khmer Rouge troops marched into the city. The brothers watched in shock as the Cambodian Republic soldiers threw down their guns and removed their uniforms at the sight of the Khmer Rouge. Chamron couldn't believe how helpless they looked standing in white shorts and t-shirts, waving white flags of surrender. Chamron turned his face from this solemn sight of despair and defeat. A wave of fear swept over him.

The brothers wanted to stay longer in Anlongville Village to watch more of the gathering troops, but they felt they should return home. On the way back through Battambang City, many military trucks and tanks surrounded them. Khmer Rouge soldiers, both inside and on top of the trucks, shouted "Victory!" and sprayed bullets into the air. Their screaming cheers were terrifying.

Most of the Khmer Rouge soldiers had never driven vehicles of any kind. Chamron witnessed soldiers driving out of control and careening into pedestrians, trees, and other motorists. Both soldiers and innocent bystanders were at risk of being killed or injured. Chamron viewed the chaos in disbelief. Getting home became most urgent.

Once home, Chamron felt safe again. But now their only source of information was the radio. What was going on? When would Mother and Darab return from Phnom Penh? What would happen to their family? They fell asleep not knowing what the morning would bring.

The next morning, there was another national radio announcement: "Every family in every village will celebrate the victory with feasts to welcome the Khmer Rouge troops. Schools, government offices, and businesses will be closed for this event. You must prepare meals to share with the soldiers who will come into your homes today."

Chamron and his siblings usually started every morning by going to mass at the nearby Catholic church. Today, they'd decided to stay home. Chamron and his brothers crowded around the radio hoping to hear more news. Narin, his oldest sister, left to buy meat, fish, and vegetables for the celebration meal. Grandma Rang and the other sisters cleaned the house for the expected guests.

Full of apprehension, the family prepared the meal for the soldiers. The sisters chopped and prepared ingredients. Grandma Rang cooked. The fragrances of each dish filled the house. Chicken soup with lemon grass, herbs, and limes with a large pot of steamed rice; Chinese broccoli with beef in black bean sauce; fried fish with sweet and sour sauce, pineapple, and green pepper; and stir-fried pork with green beans.

Government orders to host the soldiers had to be obeyed. They had to feed the intruders, but they refused to eat or celebrate with them.

Not long after they'd set the food out on the table, a group of soldiers marched into the house. They smiled and greeted the family with polite bows. The soldiers chatted and laughed amongst themselves while helping themselves to the food. The family stood outside and watched through the doorway. After a few hours, the soldiers grabbed their weapons and departed without a word—no appreciation, no thank you. Chamron's family rushed into the house. No food was left. They prepared a small meal and ate in silence.

Chamron had an unsettled feeling. What was happening? Were these strangers really their friends? They reminded him of tigers, with claws that only appear during an attack.

Later that day, the national radio made another announcement: "Our Prince Norodom Sihanouk is returning to our country. Every government official must go to a local elementary school to prepare to welcome him." Chamron cheered at the good news of the Prince's return. He hoped that life would be peaceful and normal again.

***

Prince Norodom Sihanouk became king of Cambodia in 1941 at the age of 19. He was eventually appointed to many different political offices. During his on-again, off-again reign, which ended in 1970, he befriended local Communist leaders and showed support for the Khmer Rouge.

A coup on March 18, 1970 changed the political leadership. Cambodia was declared a Republic to be led by President Lon Nol. Reigning Prince Sihanouk escaped and fled to China and North Korea. After the victory of the Khmer Rouge in 1975, the prince returned to Cambodia.

The announcement of the prince's return brought gladness to the Cambodian people. They remembered him as their leader during a long period of peace. Many were unaware of how his support of the Khmer Rouge had allowed the Communist group to grow in power and numbers. They'd heard rumors of civilians making money selling weapons, food, and supplies to them, but were unaware of their military growth and threatening plans. And they were unaware of the immense bloodshed during the eight-year civil war, which ended in Khmer Rouge's victory over Lon Nol's government on April 17, 1975.

***

Huge crowds gathered at the schools—former government officials, soldiers of all ranks, even some civilians blended in by wearing regime uniforms bought in the marketplace. They'd surrendered their weapons and official uniforms the day before.

Some of Chamron's relatives and friends, including his great uncle, put on marketplace uniforms and walked to a nearby school. They obediently followed Khmer Rouge orders, despite not knowing the new leadership's plans for Cambodia.

Chamron rode his bicycle to his childhood school, expecting to see a noisy scene of celebration. The school was full of people, but they were not celebrating. When he peeked into the classrooms, he witnessed all the former regime leaders whispering amongst themselves. Fear and anxiety filled their faces. He did not find his relatives. They must have been at another school. Chamron considered continuing his search, but distress kept him from going on. He wouldn't learn the gruesome details of what had happened that day until several years later.

Chamron jumped onto his bicycle and pedaled home. Grandma Rang met him at the door. "Did you find anyone?"

"No. They must have gone to another school," Chamron responded. "There were many people there, but none of them celebrated. They all sat in silence while Khmer Rouge soldiers stood around them armed with guns. I'm worried about Mom and Darab in Phnom Penh. I wish they were here with us."

Grandma Rang took control and led Chamron inside. "We will hold them in prayer tonight. Let us get some rest now and wait to hear more news on the radio tomorrow."

CHAPTER 2

....

SEARCHING FOR SAFE SHELTER

April 1975

For a while, life in Battambang City continued as usual. Villagers carried on with their business like nothing had happened. The value of Cambodian money, called riel, increased. People found plummeting marketplace prices and good bargains. Chamron's family bought food and household supplies at low costs.

But then one morning, another announcement issued from the national radio news station: "Everyone must leave the cities immediately. Go into the jungles and deep forest. If you do not, the American airplanes will kill you with bombs."

Chamron's mind froze in shock at the news. Almost immediately, Battambang erupted in chaos around him. People ran from their homes in terror. Chamron could not form words to express his disbelief.

Shortly after the announcement, Noe called a family meeting. After their father's death, Noe had become head of the household. Since then, Chamron had watched his brother step up and lead the family.

Back in high school, Noe got his first Bible and Christian materials from a Gideon minister who had a table set up outside the school. Chamron often saw Noe reading the Bible, but he never talked with his family about what he read. Then, in 1970, Noe attended college and studied to be a translator for a Christian relief organization. He dedicated his life to helping the poor. He played the piano for the church choir, where he met his girlfriend, Sokhorn. They loved one another, but her mother wouldn't agree to their marriage. She wanted her daughter to marry a rich man.

During the family meeting, Grandpa Nguon Seng and Grandma Rang San sat with Chamron and his siblings as they listened carefully to Noe. The brothers were Noe, age twenty-four; Nareth, nineteen; Nara, eighteen; Chamron, seventeen; Prakab, fifteen; Kosal, fourteen; and Sambath, who was seven. The sisters were: Narin, age twenty-two; Narith, twenty; Pratna, ten; and Sokha, three.

"We must follow the orders to leave the city," Noe said. "We may become separated. But when everything returns to normal, we will meet back in French Village. Does everyone understand?"

"We understand," they replied in unison.

Lugging a heavy load in the hot season was not possible, so the family heaped food and cooking supplies into a wooden wagon. Next, they grabbed backpacks and hurried to fill them to the brim with canteens, clothing, and medicines. All over Battambang City, families were doing the same. In the confusion, villagers scattered in different directions.

Narin, the oldest sister, took her infant son and went with her husband's family to Omany Village. A short time later, Noe gathered the siblings and their grandparents, and they went to meet Narin.

The grandparents set a slow pace in the heat. The entire family endured a miserable day of walking along with the crowds evacuating Battambang City. They spoke very little. With a million people jamming the roadway, their focus was spent trying to keep the family together.

Noe led the family to Narin's in-laws' shelter in Omany Village. They expected to be welcomed and have a restful place to stay. As soon as they arrived, they fell to the ground in exhaustion.

"You cannot remain here," Narin cried when she saw them. "The Cambodian Democratic government made a new regulation. Only a certain number of families are allowed in each village. They have declared this village full."

With little other choice, the family lay down outside and tried to sleep, despite the noise and congestion of thousands of other travelers. They knew they would wake up to face another day of hiking.

***

After a restless night, the weary group packed up. They plodded on through the rice fields in the hundred-degree heat. The ground was uneven and cracked, and the swarm of travelers around them kicked dust into Chamron's face. His feet were blistered, and they ached. Forcing one foot in front of the other, the family stumbled toward the forest. In the late afternoon, they finally plopped down under some shady trees to rest.

A young man traveling alone walked past them. He dropped his two bags and fell on top of them.

"What's in your bags?" Chamron asked.

"Money," the young man said.

"What? No food or supplies?" Chamron responded.

Holding up the bag of money, the man replied, "This is all I need. Soldiers forced me to leave my business in the marketplace. I had no time to go home. I will buy supplies with this."

Chamron was puzzled by his response. Didn't this man realize there was no place to buy anything in the forest?

Chamron recalled the bustling marketplace where his mother and grandmother had an open-air stall. There, they sold flat-noodle soup and vegetables from a wood burning stove. Sometimes he'd help by washing the dirty glass plates and drying them for the next customers. Sometimes people with no money came to their table and reached out their hands for soup. Chamron would watch his mother feed the beggars.

Sitting under a tree with his whole life strapped to his back, Chamron shook his head to chase away the memory. It was too painful to think of these commonplace routines now.

After they'd rested, Chamron and his family continued on their journey. The decision had been made to walk to his Great Auntie Choeurn's village.

Through the humid April heat, the family trudged along a paved road by the river. At the end of another long day, Great Auntie Choeurn welcomed the family into her home in Takok Village.

***

The next morning Auntie Choeurn walked to the village headquarters. When she returned, her face had changed. Something was wrong.

"The village leaders . . . They said you can't stay," she told them.

"Why not?" Noe pleaded. "We have nowhere else to go."

Auntie's eyes filled with tears. "They said the village is full. They told me you must leave today."

Again Chamron and his family gathered their belongings, and in despair left Auntie's home. Again, the roads teemed with travelers searching for a place to stay. The intense heat and humidity were hardest on young children, babies, the elderly, and the sick. Chamron could not count all the people lying on the side of the road, dying.

Chamron's family traveled to Tahen Village to look for their friend Mr. Chey, who had relocated from French Village last year. Five years ago, they'd met Mr. Chey and his family when they needed help. "We have come from the forest and do not know anyone here," Mr. Chey had told Chamron's father. "We escaped from the Khmer Rouge. The six of us have faced difficulties on our journey and need a place to live."

Chamron's father, Phallay, agreed to let Mr. Chey's family move in. The wooden house on stilts had a spacious ground floor where the Cheys lived in comfort. Chamron's family lived upstairs in a room lined with three mattresses divided by curtains for privacy. Outside of this shelter was a small building with two sections. One side served as the kitchen and the end toward the street had a water jar used as the bathroom. The Cheys lived with them until they saved enough to move out a few years later.

Chamron's family had a reputation for extending kindness to people in need. For a while, another family had resided upstairs with Chamron's. Non and his wife Sakhon had a three-wheel tricycle called a tuk. Non made his living transporting people around the village. The couple shared the upstairs living space with Chamron's family for a few months, with curtains dividing the single room for privacy. They all lived in peace as one large family.

Growing up, Chamron never realized his parents had financial difficulties. His father's army career provided a small income. Chamron's mother paid annually for each of her children to go to school. She didn't tell anyone that she borrowed money from friends and relatives to pay daily expenses. All twelve children attended school and worked to help support the family. Seven days a week, his mother labored long hours. She never rested nor took time for herself.

Chamron's maternal grandpa, Nguon Seng, helped support the family. This charismatic Chinese man operated an odd gambling game that was popular in Cambodia. He attracted large crowds in the marketplace and encouraged them to place bets on the rainfall that day. Villagers bet on when it would rain, how much it would rain, and the time and hour it would rain. It was a complicated system that often generated good income. Every day, Nguon placed a piece of paper on a roof in the marketplace to collect the rain. If rain did come, he created a ceremony of announcing the time and amount of rain. He enjoyed presenting money to the winners. Chamron recalled Nguon's cheerful face when he'd arrive home with a fistful of money to distribute to everyone.

Gambling was popular, but caused trouble in the lives of the losers. People watched for windstorms or lightning. They listened to hear thunder. Using these weather signs, they bet large amounts of money. It was not uncommon for big losers to commit suicide. When he was young, Chamron did not know why his grandpa had periods of silence and withdrew from the family.

Later he found out that losing caused him to suffer bouts of depression. Eventually Nguon's gambling business completely collapsed. No one had money to participate in the games anymore.

When Chamron's family reached the crowded streets of Tahen Village to search for Mr. Chey, darkness was beginning to settle in. Later that night, they located him in a temporary shelter on the edge of the village.

"We can't stay here more than a day," he told them. "Tahen Village leaders are enforcing the new laws. I think we should set up our own village. Do you want to join me?"

Noe spoke for the family. "We are tired of being turned away from village after village. Your idea of a new village is a good one. We will go with you."

It was too late to keep walking, so they looked around for a place to settle for the night. Barren fields full of traumatized families surrounded a farmhouse in the distance. Buffalo, cows, and oxen grazed on one side of the barn. The stench from the animal enclosure filled the air.

Noe pinched his nose. "Pew! Let's go over to the far side of the barn."

The family made their way to an open area away from the animals. Fanning herself, Grandma said, "Gather rocks and make a fire pit." The brothers made the fire pit and created a shelter over Grandma by tying a large plastic sheet to the barn. She began to prepare the evening meal.

Chamron drew near the fire. "The food smells so good that I am no longer bothered by the animal stench."

After dinner, Chamron lay on his back, his head resting on a clump of hay. He turned to Noe and spoke quietly. "I am worried about Mom and Darab in Phnom Penh. The radio said the city was captured by the Khmer Rouge troops. Our family is scattered, and we are aliens in a strange land. We will return to our village someday, won't we?"

Noe nodded, but it didn't calm the uncertainty Chamron felt.

"But how can we find Mom and Darab? Our family needs to be together," Chamron asked.

Noe had no answer.

Overcome with exhaustion, the brothers fell into silence. Sleep soon followed.

Their future was a mystery.

CHAPTER 3

....

FROM CERTAINTY TO
CONFUSION

April 1975

From all over Cambodia people were forced to abandon their homes and relocate to fields and forests. Chamron's family joined Mr. Chey and a group of travelers, not knowing where they were heading or what to expect next. They were led by Mr. Chey's brother-in-law, Mr. Ruoy, who had orders from the Khmer Rouge to establish a new village.

As they walked, Chamron scanned the cultivated rice fields all around. He and his family trudged on for a full day until they reached a large, barren hilltop, where Mr. Chey told their group to stop. The many other travelers kept walking beyond the hilltop, looking for a place to settle as well.

As Chamron stood on the hill waiting to hear the next step in the plan, he felt something biting at his ankles. He stooped over to find the cause. "I'm covered with fleas!" Chamron yelled, frantically clawing at his sweaty legs.

Before long Mr. Chey announced, "This will be our new village. We will name it Dog Flea Village."

Chamron looked around at everyone scratching flea-bitten arms and legs. "That's a perfect name for this place."

"But wait!" someone called from the crowd. "What can we do about all these fleas biting us?"

Mr. Chey's brother-in-law, Mr. Rouy, moved toward the center of the group and took command. As they had learned, the Khmer Rouge Democratic leaders had assigned Mr. Rouy to manage their new village. "Stop complaining about the fleas," Mr. Rouy ordered. "Fires will eliminate them and make this hill a good place for us."

Getting rid of the fleas became a top priority. Mr. Rouy faced the crowd and said, "Gather the brush, grass, and vegetation on this hill. Put it into piles and burn everything. This will clear out the fleas."

Once the fires burned out and they no longer had to worry about being bitten, everyone focused on building shelters.

"Fill in all these holes and ditches to flatten the land before you start building," Mr. Rouy ordered. "Each family may select a spot to construct a shelter. You must build your own shelters before the rains come. Go into the forest and cut down trees. You can carry them back to the village. Gather vines to use as rope."

Noe led his family to a quieter place on the edge of the rice fields where rainwater had puddled. For days the men and boys hauled bundles of tree trunks, vines, and hay to Dog Flea Village. One day, as they headed into the forest, Chamron looked at his brothers and said, "Every part of my body aches. I always thought I was a hard worker, but I have never worked this hard before."

Grandma Rang and Camron's sisters set up temporary places for cooking and sleeping. They prepared meals from supplies they had carried with them and edible plants gathered from the forest.

A little way into Roneem Forest, they found Mr. Rouy. He was visibly angry. He had discovered Chamron's brother Noe was a student commando. Mr. Rouy separated Noe from his brothers. Chamron anticipated reuniting with Noe at the end of the day's work, but it got later and later, and Noe never returned. Where had he gone?

The next day, Chamron and his brothers were tasked with hauling building materials from the forest to Dog Flea Village. Once they'd gathered enough, they focused their attention on the dilemma of building without nails or wire. They eventually devised a way to tie vines to bamboo to form flooring and walls and built one large room a few feet above the ground. Chamron climbed on top and formed a roof by covering the structure with hay and palm fronds.

After two weeks of fatiguing labor, Chamron and his brother's put the finishing touches on the room. He looked over the faces of his siblings. "We did it! We built our room. And I think it is high enough to protect us from the flooding." Chamron couldn't help feeling proud, despite the fact that as each day passed without the arrival of his missing family members, his worry increased.

Chamron turned to his brother Narith. "Stack some dry wood under the shelter while the rest of us pile dirt for a kitchen room foundation."

The brothers continued working to make a kitchen room on the pile of dirt beside the big room. They dug holes to support small tree trunks in a square. Again they used vines to attach bamboo above the trunks to make a roof. Hay and palm fronds covered the sides and roof. Inside the structure, they piled stones in a triangular shape to make a stove. It took another week to finish the kitchen room. Once complete, Chamron dragged their wagon close to the new shelter and carried the scarce number of pots and dishes into the kitchen room.

Chamron's family had left Battambang in haste, without many household items. After arranging the items they had carried in a corner near the stove, he sniffed the air, then turned to his brothers. "I am pretending to smell fried bananas, roasted sweet potatoes, and amok. I see Grandma and Mother in French Village cooking delicious foods to sell in the marketplace." His mouth watered at the thought of eating some of his favorites cooked by his mother and grandmother.

Chamron's brother Nara smiled and joined in the moment of make-believe. "Amok is my favorite. I will wrap the raw fish, Chinese broccoli, lemongrass, and herbs in banana leaves. Then Mother can boil them in coconut milk."

"Yes! I will stack the amok high on my bamboo basket and carry them on my head to sell in the nearby villages," Chamron added. He and his brothers enjoyed the few moments of escape, laughing as they acted out the anticipative work of meal preparation.

Chamron stopped and released a deep breath as the truth of their reality returned. "Carrying that food was fun. Not hard like these tree trunk bundles."

The brothers sat together in silence for some time. Chamron's heart was heavy with sadness. He and his family faced drastic changes. They didn't know the whereabouts of Noe, their mother, or Darab, or even if they were safe. However short, the recollection of their wonderful times in French Village had brought them a bit of delight. These memories reminded them that they were once a family unit. And these thoughts strengthened their resolve to be together as a family again.

***

After a long and fatiguing month of labor, they'd finished building the shelters, and the village was functioning like a vital community. Chamron's family was finally able to rest and spend time together. But the harsh reality of their circumstances returned when two Khmer Rouge soldiers marched into the village one day.

"Come and listen carefully!" one of the soldier's yelled. "We have been sent by county leaders to order you to attend a mandatory meeting. Tomorrow morning, all adults must report to the center by the leaders' houses."

Uneasiness flooded back in.

The next morning, the villagers traveled two hours to a bamboo shelter equipped with microphones and speakers. Thousands of villagers had assembled on the hard ground. Armed soldiers surrounded the area. Top Khmer Rouge leaders introduced themselves before one of the county leaders began to explain the new government plan.

"We will rebuild this country together," he began, confidently. "Your future will be bright and beautiful. I will now explain the government's plan:

Everyone in the regime is equal.

Every morning you will be given fresh bread.

You are all farmers who belong to Angkar (the government).

All children will be taken away to be raised by Angkar.

Everything belongs to the government.

There is no private ownership.

We will not preserve anyone who does not bring profit to us.

No one is to mention the former regime or their past life.

All people must eat and work together as one family. Only those who work may eat.

You must produce eight tons of rice from every hundred square meters of land.

Only the Cambodian language can be spoken.

Everyone must wear black clothing.

Do not steal or you will be killed.

Music is restricted to patriotic Khmer Rouge Democratic songs.

No public displays of affection or romance.

All religious activities are prohibited.

Travel from village to village is not allowed."

The county leader paused and looked around at the crowd before continuing. He spoke in a soothing voice, but the content was clearly threatening. "The Angkar government is like a wheel moving forward quickly," he said. "If you do not roll with the government, you will be rolled over or killed. Do not stand in the way of Angkar." Smiling, he added, "Everyone who served in the Republic government, please come forward. You are going to be reinstated into your former jobs."

Without delay some people raised their hands; others hesitated before following suit.

Pointing to the group who had raised their hands, the leader said, "You stay here. The rest of you leave now and return to your work in the villages."

Chamron watched. Could these leaders be trusted? He had no way to know.

But Chamron would never see those Republic government workers again.

***

The Khmer Rouge soldiers deceived people into following their plan with promises of a good life. In reality, the rules had been designed to create total control of the Cambodians. There were many educated people in the group listening that day as the announcements were made. Until just a few weeks before, their lives had been joyful and successful. But this new government ordered them to turn their backs on their past and accept lives of slavery and hard labor.

Despite all the promises made, the following reflects what actually happened in Dog Flea Village:

Villagers were oppressed and were never equal.

They never received fresh bread.

Even after hard days of labor, they were not given adequate food.

Eating food from their small family gardens—the gardens they alone had cultivated—was considered stealing and was punishable by death.

Those who stayed behind that day—those who worked for the former government—were among the hundreds of thousands of innocent people taken away and killed. The Khmer Rouge Communists did not want to waste bullets, so they led them blindfolded to a large pit and hit them in the back of the head with bamboo rods. Not everyone died from the blow. The soldiers covered them with dirt, suffocating those still alive.

***

After the meeting that day, Chamron became more cautious. He paid close attention to all those who went away and never returned. Not a minute passed that he didn't think of his mother and siblings who were still missing.

Chamron took his family photos and looked at them one by one. The photos showed his father in his military uniform, Noe dressed as a commando, his siblings in their school uniforms, and the priests at the Catholic Church. These photos were dangerous evidence of his family's military service, education, and religious connections. With care, Chamron placed the family photos in plastic bags and tucked them away in the hay roof. The packages had to be small enough to be hidden deep in the hay. This would keep them from slipping out during the rains.

Chamron's grandfather Nguon kept the family informed by listening to his radio. He preferred a station that featured Cambodian politics in the Cambodian language. Chamron was surprised this radio was never taken away by the Khmer Rouge, but Mr. Chey liked Nguon and used his influence to convince Mr. Rouy to allow him to keep the radio.

***

Five years earlier, in 1970, former Cambodian Head of State Prince Norodom Sihanouk was overthrown by a military coup led by Lon Nol. This event led to the forming of the Khmer Republic. Soon after his removal, Sihanouk announced his support of the Khmer Rouge, which at the time was an armed Communist resistance movement led by Pol Pot.

Spurred by the upheaval and inspired by their former leader's support, many citizens voluntarily joined the Khmer Rouge to fight against the Republic. They'd expected to achieve a better life for themselves by doing so and had sacrificed everything when they left their families and professions to become soldiers. Khmer Rouge numbers swelled, and within a few months, the Khmer Rouge had gained control of the entire northeastern third of the country.

Some of the defectors remained in their jobs and worked undercover for the Khmer Rouge. Several of Chamron's high school professors worked as spies during the revolution. In 1975, Chamron was shocked when he saw his teachers now dressed in black uniforms working with the Khmer Rouge.

By the time the Khmer Rouge took control of Phnom Penh in 1975, Chamron, Nara, and Nareth had each completed three years of high school. The previous government had required students to learn how to protect the school from an enemy attack. Their first school year, they received military training. His father did not want his children to join the army, but Chamron had dreamed of being a soldier. He'd envied his brother Noe, who was a commando and had a gun, bayonet, and a canteen—all made in the United States. From 1970 to 1975, the US government was a friend of Cambodia and provided the Republic government led by Lon Nol with food, supplies, weapons, tanks, aircraft, and military training.

After the 1975 takeover, the civilians with no Khmer Rouge background were called "April 17" (the day that the Khmer Rouge took command of Cambodia). All Chamron's family and people from French Village were given this label.

The group leaders conducted background checks using forms that asked for personal information. In order to protect themselves, everyone lied about their occupations and religious affiliations. Connections with the Republic government, businesses, or higher education had to be hidden. Villagers had to appear to be poor farmers.

***

"Come help me," Chamron called to Narith and Nara. "We must follow the Communist government's orders and dye all our clothing black. They said the colorful clothes are reminders of the past and will corrupt our minds."

Narith and Nara began the process by boiling dong kor fruit until the water turned black. They dipped the bright clothes one by one into the dark mixture and handed the wet clothes to Chamron. Pointing to a sunny spot, Narith said, "Bury these clothes over there in the mud. The wet mud will help set the dye."

Chamron dyed his father's uniform shirt and pants with the big pockets. He loved wearing those old pants.

They waited two days for the clothing to turn black. The beauty of their colorful Cambodian clothing was stripped away. All was black. This darkness filled Chamron with sadness.

That night, Chamron's family was disturbed when they heard a person crawling under their shelter. Chamron peeked through a crack in the bamboo floor and saw a Khmer Rouge soldier listening to their conversation. He poured hot water into the crack onto the head of the intruder and chuckled as the man ran away screaming.

Khmer Rouge soldiers and village leaders observed everything that happened in Dog Flea Village and reported back to the Communist government. Chamron's family realized they had no privacy, even in their own shelter. Their words, like their hidden photos, could endanger their lives. They couldn't speak about their past nor complain about their current circumstances. They would now have to be mindful of every conversation.

One never knew when the tiger was hiding in the shadows.

CHAPTER 4

....

FROM FREEDOM TO
FORCED LABOR

May 1975

Chamron watched and listened as the Khmer
Rouge soldiers interrogated each of the 150 families
in Dog Flea Village. They separated the family units
and sent some adults into the fields to plow and others
to grind rice into flour using primitive instruments.
Some of Chamron's younger friends were taken away
in buses. The soldiers said they were going to a good
life in orphanages.

Chamron helped Grandma Rang and the older
women gather the youngest who were left in the village.
They tried to calm the frightened children by holding
them and showing them love. The Khmer Rouge had
no respect for the senior citizens who remained in
the village. They suffered from mistreatment, disease,
and starvation. Chamron observed the Khmer Rouge

walking the weakest old women into the forest. Like so many others, they were never seen again.

Every day, Chamron's grandfather Nguon joined a group of older men in a central shelter where they produced medicines. They'd walk deep into the forest to gather tree roots, herbs, turtles, and honey. In their hunger, the men would devour the turtle meat in the forest before carrying back the shells. Before the soldiers could take all the meat and leave them none. When they'd return, Chamron would watch them make pills from the leftover turtle shells following an ancient method passed down over many years. They'd grind the shells into fine particles and mix in honey and water to form a paste. They'd spread this paste on the flat ground and repeatedly poke it with a sharp, circle-shaped tool to make pills. Before being stored in jars, the small pills were shaken in a basket and left to dry. Honey mixed with herbs and roots made different pills. Chamron did not know if these ancient medicines possessed any healing powers, but he liked the sweet taste of the honey. And villagers had no access to modern medicines.

In another section of Dog Flea Village, men used bamboo frames covered with cement to make grinders. They needed grinders to crush both dry grains and ancient medicinal ingredients. In preparation for cooking, women used the grinders to separate rice grain from the scale.

Chamron liked to carry the bamboo baskets that the men made in different sizes for use throughout the village, but he had little time to watch the men weaving them. Each day he was interrupted by guards, who forced him into a line with one hundred other young men. They were each given a bucket and forced to walk for hours in oppressive heat to a deep pond in Panha Village, then made to haul buckets of water for hours into the night.

"These buckets of water are too heavy for us to carry over and over every night," one man complained.

No one responded.

Night after night the weary men repeated the difficult journey, hauling heavy buckets of water.

Eventually, the Communist leaders decided constructing a pond in Dog Flea Village would solve the water problem. They gathered Chamron's unit of young adults, and one of them pointed to a large, dry patch of ground and said, "We want a pond here. Start digging. Fill these baskets with dirt. Move quickly. You must complete the pond before the June rains begin."

Chamron's group had no shovels or tools of any kind. They dug the parched earth with their bare hands and little by little filled the large bamboo baskets. In the blazing heat, they labored at a steady pace and passed baskets of dirt from man to man to form the pond sides. No rest was allowed. Following days of digging, they faced evenings of hauling water.

After countless days of digging, a 100-square-meter hole was created. But the need for water in Dog Flea Village would not be resolved until rain filled the pond.

One of the leaders proudly declared, "This hole is ready for water. Now you villagers must haul water and fill it up. In June, the monsoon rains will come and make it a pond."

The lives of Cambodian farmers were centered around three distinct seasons. The rice planting season began in May and lasted until August. The waiting period for the rice to grow was from September to November. Harvest began in late November and continued through January. From February to May, the farmers planted beans and potatoes. Cambodia was blessed with rich, fertile land for growing rice and other crops.

With the pond construction complete, Chamron's group was sent out to prepare land for rice planting. Chamron, Narith, Nara, and Prakab headed toward the bumpy, dry ground adjacent to Dog Flea Village. They shook their heads in disbelief at what they were ordered to do.

"This thick grass has deep roots. How are we supposed to dig it up with just our hands?" Chamron asked Nara.

"Other teenagers are in the forest burning down trees and planting rice," he told him. "None of us have easy jobs."

"It's planting season. That means it is my birthday month! I will be eighteen and I want to celebrate with a day off." Chamron sighed. "I know it is not possible, but I can wish for it."

"Chamron, be quiet," Nara scolded. "We must get back to work." Then, a moment later, he turned and whispered, "Happy birthday."

Just when they thought conditions could not get worse, rains flooded the untilled dirt, turning it into a muddy marsh. Slushing through the mud, they attempted to prepare the soil for planting. The humidity made their bodies drip with sticky sweat.

Farmers in Cambodia conscientiously maintained their fields year to year. These efforts prevented the monsoons from interfering with their planting season. But this land had not been managed. It was backbreaking work for Chamron and his brothers to dig the muddy, unfarmed land.

The leadership grew impatient with the slow progress Chamron and the other men made in getting the field ready for rice planting. Eventually the Khmer Rouge gave them oxen to assist in plowing the earth to speed up the process. Part of the work became easier in June when heavy rain filled the pond. Chamron was grateful that he no longer had to take long walks and haul water every night. After the monsoon rains, dark-green morning glories began growing in the rice fields.

One evening Chamron and his brothers returned to their shelter in Dog Flea Village with armfuls of morning glories. The wild morning glories had long stems covered with leaves. Both the stems and leaves were filled with vitamins and protein. Grandma Rang chopped the long stems into tiny pieces and boiled them. She squeezed out the water and mixed the stem bits with rice to make a thick porridge. The leaves and some stems were reserved for a later dish of thin broth without rice. Grandma Rang was an excellent cook who knew how to prepare flavorful meals using meager ingredients.

"Grandma, this porridge is delicious," Chamron exclaimed as he finished his fourth bowlful. Suddenly he grabbed his stomach and doubled over with cramps. Sobbing he ran into a nearby field.

Chamron moaned as he experienced severe diarrhea. In his hunger, he'd made the mistake of eating too much at once. Fortunately, his family had brought some modern medicines in their backpacks when they left French Village. Chamron's dysentery was quickly relieved by the medicines.

***

In Dog Flea Village, no one had a watch or a calendar. Bells and whistles regulated their lives. Every day at 4:00 a.m., Chamron heard a whistle and leaped to his feet to avoid punishment. He got no breakfast, but trekked in a line to the rice fields. Due to extreme fatigue, he often marched with his eyes closed. His head hanging, he watched for his shadow to fall below his feet. This signaled noontime, and he knew he would soon get to eat.

Following a morning of strenuous labor, Chamron would eat his first meal of the day in the community kitchen at a long table under the shade of a grass and hay roof. Villagers on the cook team fixed lunch. The small meal never satisfied his hunger.

The blazing sun heated the water in the rice fields. Wading into the shallows, Chamron watched a crab climb onto a rice plant. He reached out and grabbed the crab and gave out a loud cheer. "Look what I caught! That silly crab made it easy for me to capture him!" It was so hot that day, thousands of crabs appeared all over the field, clinging to the rice plants.

Usually, at dinnertime, they took the skimpy portions of food they were given to their shelters, where they added a few nutritious ingredients found in the field. They scavenged in the fields for morning glories, snails, snakes, frogs, crickets, fish, and rats. The rats in the rice fields were big and delicious—not like the city rats that ate sewage. But this evening, the starving villagers feasted on crab.

By the end of June, distribution of rice rations ceased Everyone moved from hunger to starvation. After working ten hours a day as farmers, the villagers were required to attend nightly propaganda meetings. The mandatory gatherings were held on a dirt area surrounded by loudspeakers. Hiding behind people and sleeping was common during these assemblies. This night, Chamron's head bobbed, and he awoke when his body jerked forward. Thankfully he hadn't fallen. Guards surveying the crowd beat anyone caught sleeping.

The rigorous daily agenda sapped Chamron's strength. He never experienced a refreshing night's sleep. He spoke less and less. Partly from exhaustion, but also in fear of saying something that would anger the guards. Besides, it took all his energy simply to survive day to day.

During the night meeting the next day, one of the Communist leaders scolded the group saying, "You must work harder. No talking is allowed. Stop complaining and pretending to be sick."

Without thinking, Chamron jumped to his feet. He faced the leaders and declared with boldness, "We work hard all day in the wet fields. You leaders stand on dry land and smoke and yell and point fingers at us."

Immediately, Chamron realized his words could cost him his life. He sat down and tried to hide in the crowd. When the meeting ended, two Khmer Rouge Communist leaders marched into the throng and grabbed Chamron by his arms. One of the men shouted, "How dare you speak against our Angkar. You are a troublemaker!"

Chamron responded in a quiet voice, "Comrade, I said it because you told us we are equal and can expect fair treatment from you. Don't you see that we are sick? We need food and rest."

The two men dragged Chamron from the meeting place to the leaders' large shelter. They shoved him into a narrow space below the shelter. He was forced to lie on his back with his face nearly touching the bottom of the bamboo floor. His body ached as he lay in the tight space. His face was crushed as the men in the room above walked back and forth. Some of these leaders had been students with him during the Republic. Now that they had positions of authority, they'd changed. They showed no compassion or respect for past friends.

The next morning, Chamron was told to crawl out from under the shelter. He stretched his aching arms and legs. His body throbbed as he stood on his cramped legs. A guard shoved his back and yelled, "Get back to work."

Later that day, he glanced at a soldier and recognized his precious Bible. He shuddered when he saw the man use the thin Bible pages to make cigarettes.

Once in a while, after the night meetings, soldiers distributed small amounts of tobacco. Chamron observed the smokers lining up to take piles of tobacco from a long table. He walked over and tried to grab some tobacco that he could save and later exchange for food.

"Stop! Do you smoke?" a Communist leader demanded.

Chamron answered, "No."

"Then you cannot have any tobacco," the leader said.

Chamron decided it would be advantageous to become a smoker. Smokers were allowed to take periodic breaks. This was the only time of rest from the hard labor. He learned to roll tobacco in pages from books his friends had. Later, he used large leaves that he'd flattened by sleeping on them. The flat leaves softened when put in the sun. This made them easier to roll.

He choked and struggled when he first started smoking. It was not as pleasant as he expected it to be. He felt good once he could smoke without choking. He wondered how people got the smoke to come out of their nose. He wanted to do that. He practiced until he could easily blow smoke out his nose while participating in the smoke breaks.

The Communists demanded many Cambodians to work night shifts to complete work more quickly. Chamron was in a group selected to miss the mandatory night meetings and work in the fields at night. Working both day and night was unbearable. Some of Chamron's friends developed a trick to avoid night work. They made up an eye disease they called "chicken blindness." They explained that chickens cannot see at night and some people have this condition as well. At night, Communist leaders tested them by making them walk barefoot over thorns to prove blindness. If they walked around the thorns it was clear they had lied. While painful, walking on the thorns was one way to get out of the night shift.

Chamron worked night and day until his body collapsed from exhaustion. Malnourishment caused his legs to swell. The constant demand to trudge many kilometers over wet land weakened his legs. Once he could no longer stand or walk, he was told to leave the field. With his entire body wet from constant rain, he sat on the edge of the rice field and wondered what would happen to him.

Brief breaks from work never restored his energy. Both his body and mind became numb from fatigue. He could hardly think at all. His former life was dim— like a distant memory. To survive, he needed all the strength his eighteen-year-old body could produce.

CHAPTER 5

....

SURVIVING STARVATION

July 1975

While sitting on the edge of the rice field resting his swollen legs, Chamron reminisced about his childhood days in Battambang City. The rich memories filled his mind with vivid pictures of his school days. Despite his misery, Chamron could not help but smile when he remembered the time when, on his first day of school, he'd fallen through the bamboo ceiling of his home. This is how it happened:

Uncle Song was one of the orphans raised by Chamron's grandparents. Even in his thirties, Uncle Song liked to watch cartoons at the movie theater and read comic books. But he wanted to be helpful, so he walked with Chamron on his first day of school.

Little Chamron was terrified by the thought of going to first grade. He shook when Uncle Song left him near the classroom. When Uncle Song was out of sight, Chamron turned and ran from the school grounds. Once or twice he looked over his shoulder to check that no one followed him. He saw no one, but he kept on running until he reached the marketplace.

Wandering around the marketplace made him tired, so he crept back into his house and crawled into a tiny space in the ceiling. His plan to hide there the rest of the day failed when he knelt on some bamboo poles stored in the ceiling. The poles slipped and tossed him through the ceiling. His body crashed through the ceiling onto the wooden floor below.

Uncle Song, hearing the noise, ran into the room. "Who is there?" Upon discovering Chamron lying on the floor in pain, he said, "You are supposed to be in school! What are you doing here?"

"I don't want to go to school," Chamron replied. "I want to stay here with you." Pain from the fall faded, but not Chamron's emotional pain.

The next day, Uncle Song escorted Chamron back to school and waited with him until the door opened. He grabbed the boy by the arm and pulled him into the classroom. Uncle Song approached the teacher and said, "I want you to meet Chamron. He ran away from school yesterday. Watch that he does not leave today."

This news angered Chamron's teacher. Once Uncle Song left, she grabbed a branch leaning by her desk and punished the boy with blows to the palms of his hands until they were covered with red stripes. His loud screams filled the classroom. Chamron rubbed his hands on his pants. They stung and hurt all day. The pain was so severe that he never again missed a day of school.

Being quiet and sitting in school was hard for Chamron. He was an active boy who liked to run around outside all day. Before going to school, nobody had taken the time to explain to him how to count or what numbers meant. The loud group chanting numbers and doing simple calculations confused him. In the class of fifty students, not one person noticed his struggles nor offered to help him.

He got poor scores in first grade. Many of his papers had zeros marked on them. Uncle Song teased him about the zeros and drew on his papers, turning the zeros into eyeglasses.

Chamron's parents loved him, but lost contact when the army transferred his father from Battambang to Phnom Penh. The eleven children remained separated from their parents for five years. Chamron lived with his grandparents, who never noticed his lack of success in school. They met his basic needs by keeping a roof over his head and feeding him.

Despite his failing performance, Chamron was passed to second grade. His promotion was based on his perfect attendance. He developed an interest in learning in second grade and did well after that first year. Chamron was proficient in languages and turned out to be a good communicator—speaking both Cambodian and French. He was a popular student and excelled at ping pong, which he played on the school yard every day during class breaks.

Chamron's third-grade teacher, Mr. Thy, tortured him nearly every day that school year. Mr. Thy had just instructed the students to take turns reading lines of a long paragraph written on the chalkboard when he noticed Chamron chatting with a friend. He moved toward the student who was reading and shouted, "Stop right there!" He poked Chamron with a meter stick and said, "You continue reading now."

Chamron looked at the board and blinked his eyes. He had no idea where to begin reading.

Mr. Thy motioned him to come to his desk. He led him to a pile of jackfruit on the ground near his desk and grumbled, "Kneel on that spikey fruit."

Chamron obeyed. His thick khaki pants gave him a little protection from the thorns. But after a short time, he experienced sharp stinging in his knees. He struggled as he remained in that position for the entire period—over an hour.

Another time after Chamron misbehaved, Mr. Thy ordered him to lie on the dirt floor. The teacher shouted, "Move your arms and legs in a swimming motion."

Chamron moved as instructed and cried out, "Ouch! This is scratching my chest. My legs hurt." When Mr. Thy turned away, Chamron stuffed paper under his shirt.

"What is making that crinkling sound?" asked Mr. Thy. Looking around, he yelled, "Chamron, come here." When Chamron approached him, he grabbed the paper out of his shirt and hit him on his back with a bamboo rod.

Mr. Thy was the only teacher who ever poked Chamron's hands and head with a sharp pen when he made math errors. The poked spots eventually became raw and itchy. Chamron trembled in fear every time Mr. Thy called him to his desk, knowing he would have to endure a painful punishment.

Because of the overthrow of the government in 1975, Chamron's schooling ended a few months before he was able to graduate high school. All education in Cambodia stopped once the invading Communist Khmer Rouge forced families out of the cities.

***

Chamron would have given anything to be back in school suffering the simple punishments that now seemed silly. Instead he faced the harsh reality of starvation that threatened everyone in Dog Flea Village. The Khmer Rouge leaders watched as hunger reached critical levels. In order to preserve the labor force, they had to devise a way to feed them.

Mr. Rouy gathered the villagers and announced, "Anlongville Village has a grain factory. Members from each family must take bags and bamboo carriers and collect rice scale from the factory."

Men in Dog Flea Village had made special bamboo carriers to use when transporting objects. They sliced twelve-centimeter diameter bamboo rods vertically to begin the process. The knots were cut off and smoothed to flatten the poles. A curved knot was preserved on each end of the two-meter shafts to prevent loads from slipping. The long poles were flexible and bounced on their shoulders as they walked. This movement produced brief moments of relief from pressure on their shoulders. These handmade poles were valuable and would be stolen if left outside the shelter.

The abandoned Anlongville grain factory had once made livestock feed. This factory separated the white rice grains from the brown covering (the scale) and ground them into flour. The moment Chamron and Nara reached the factory, they rushed forward with enthusiasm. They had no idea the bags had been stored for years and contained tiny insects. Grabbing handfuls of scale and insects, they sat and gobbled them up. Drinking water from the nearby water jars kept them from choking on the dry scale.

"I cannot explain it, but this is tasty!" Chamron said.

Nara nodded his head in agreement as he chewed the dry scale.

They ate until their stomachs felt full.

The brothers each balanced two bags of scale on their bamboo poles and rested them on their shoulders.

They carried a third bag on their backs. The loads weighed heavily on their thin bodies. Staggering under the weight, they shuffled along the path back toward the village.

Chamron squirmed in pain as insects crawled out of the bags and bit him. The bugs covered his sweaty back and arms as he walked the several kilometers to Dog Flea Village, but he had no hands free to swat the insects off his body.

Chamron's sister, Narith, ran down the road and grabbed one of the bags. She hugged her brothers. "Thank you for bringing us this food. Now we will not starve."

Back at their shelter, Narith separated the scale from the insects. "I know I can make the scale into a tasty treat," she told them. She had learned by watching Grandma Rang cook many different dishes.

She mixed the scale with water and salt and wrapped the little cakes in banana leaves. A sweet aroma filled the air as the cakes cooked over the burning wood. Chamron smelled the air and remarked, "How delicious that bread smells. What a feast!"

After they'd eaten, Chamron considered that in the past, they'd used scale to feed pigs. He'd never dreamed that one day he would delight in eating pig food like the Prodigal Son in the Bible.

By August, more people had died from starvation, and the workforce shrank due to the increasing deaths. The leadership decided to send a group to the county leaders' rice storage in Panha Village. Chamron and Nara were among those selected to get rice for Dog Flea Village. Chamron changed into his father's military pants that had many pockets.

The worn-out villagers hiked five kilometers over rough terrain to Panha Village. The journey took a long time, because they were exhausted and had to walk around a series of wet rice fields. The few roads along the way were unpaved and muddy.

At noon, they arrived at the storage units. The men rushed toward the huge bags of rice. The rice was raw, but they did not care. Immediately, they ate handfuls and drank water. The water swelled the raw rice in their stomachs. Some men got sick from doing this. Fortunately, Chamron and Nara did not get ill.

After putting down his bamboo carrier, Chamron loaded rice into his three bags. He stumbled as he tried to move forward with the hefty bags on the bamboo carrier and a bag on his back. He stuffed more rice into the military pants pockets. His family was counting on him to bring home as much rice as possible. Nara shared Chamron's resolve. He struggled with an identical burden.

The entire group slugged along and stopped many times to rest. When it got dark, Chamron transferred rice from his pockets into an extra bag and hid it in the forest. He knew the greedy leadership planned to take all the rice he was carrying. When they arrived at the village, he followed orders and dropped the rice bundles in the center of the village. Then he rushed back to the forest and retrieved the hidden bag of precious rice. Grandma Rang knew how to prepare porridge to stretch that rice into many meals.

This time of widespread famine forced Chamron to make one of the hardest decisions of his life. His ten-year-old dog had been living with him in Dog Flea Village. Every time Chamron came home, his dog greeted him with his tail wagging and covered him with wet licks. His heart pounded in his chest the day he took his dog behind their shelter and hit him with a bamboo rod. Tears poured down his face as he killed his dear dog to feed his family. Years later, he could still hear his dog screaming as he took its life. There was a small comfort in knowing the Khmer Rouge would have eventually taken his dog away and eaten it.

The weakened workers were not allowed to rest after they finished planting rice. The Khmer Rouge leaders kept them busy planting other fields with potatoes, sugar cane, and vegetables. They had to maintain the same long hours of work—again without proper nourishment. Chamron's family managed to survive for months, even without rice. They performed forced labor and searched daily for something to feed the family.

When working in the fields, Chamron wore his pants with no pockets. His father's military pants with pockets were too hot and bulky to wear every day. His goal each day was to fill his waistband with one or two crabs, snails, fish, or frogs—anything to feed his starving family.

One day, while looking for food, one of the crabs Chamron had caught crawled out of his waistband and pinched his stomach. "Yipes!" he cried. He grabbed the crab and threw it on the ground, but then stuffed it back in his waistband.

Miraculously Chamron managed to find something to eat every day—even items he never considered "food" before the Khmer Rouge invasion. For the first time, he tasted lizards, crickets, and snakes.

During the October waiting period, Nara and Chamron formed a plan based on the fact that the Khmer Rouge soldiers could not read. Being educated, the brothers had no problem drafting the following letter:

I am a Dog Flea Village leader. I grant permission for these two men to travel to Rokar Village to visit their brother Nareth and bring back food supplies.

They signed the note with the name of Mr. Rouy, their leader.

That night they took the letter and followed a specific route to Rokar Village—one which avoided patrolling soldiers. After traveling three hours, they reached Nareth's shelter and rested until morning. At first light, they presented their letter to the Rokar Village leaders. The leaders held the letter upside down and ordered, "Read this letter to us."

Chamron and Nara had to be courageous and confident in front of these leaders. This hazardous plan could result in death. Upon hearing the letter and realizing the food was for Mr. Rouy, the leaders agreed and allowed them to continue their journey. The validity of the letter was never questioned. They repeated this successful scheme several times over the next months. It was dangerous, but they took the risk for their family's survival.

On their first trip to Rokar Village, Chamron was shocked to find Noe there. He never knew Noe had escaped and was living with Nareth. Noe explained how some sympathetic leaders had helped him elude the execution ordered by Mr. Rouy.

The November harvest season arrived, and for a short time Chamron's family had rice and relief from starvation. But their troubles did not end, despite the food. Mr. Chey's cousin began asking about the family's background. Mr. Chey, not realizing his cousin was just looking for information he could use to gain favor with the Khmer Rouge government, told him all about Chamron's family. The cousin then betrayed them by reporting their military, religious, and educational history. Everyone knew the Khmer Rouge used this kind of information to isolate and label families as enemies of the new government.

One night in December, Noe and Nareth left Rokar Village and crept back into Dog Flea Village to warn their family. Noe got right to the point.

"Mr. Chey's cousin has betrayed you. Because of information he has shared with the Khmer Rouge government, our family has been identified as an enemy. They intend to get rid of you. Nareth and I have a plan to obtain permission for your relocation to Rokar Village. We need to get you out of here as soon as possible."

Nareth added to the urgency by telling them about their friend, Mr. An.

"I need to tell you, Mr. An is dead. Remember how he protected us from disruptive strangers who tried to cause trouble in French Village? The Khmer Rouge saw the Air Force tattoo on his shoulder. They beat him and dragged him into the forest. In secret, I followed them. They took off his clothes, bound him with rope, and stretched his body to make an X. They bayonetted him and left him to bleed to death. Your lives are in danger; now they will come to kill you. Noe and I must return to Rokar Village, but we will come back for you as soon as we can."

Chamron shuddered with disgust and terror after hearing of the betrayal of his family and the horrific killing of Mr. An. The brutality toward his friend enraged him and left him shaken. He understood it was no longer safe to stay in Dog Flea with his friends from French Village. He helped get his family ready to move.

Fear mounted as they waited and waited for Noe to return to Dog Flea Village to escort them to Rokar Village. Every night they expected him to come back.

Finally, three weeks later in January 1976, Noe and Nareth managed to sneak back into Dog Flea Village. They were met by the assistant leaders who had been kind to the family. One of the leaders warned them saying, "You are lucky Mr. Rouy is not here tonight. But he may return at any time. You must leave before he comes back."

The brothers hurried to Chamron's shelter and urged the family to move without delay. There was no time to rest and spend the night. Chamron's family members gathered their packed bags and rushed out in the cover of darkness to begin the three-hour walk to Rokar Village. Nine months had passed since they were forced to leave their home and move to Dog Flea Village. They thought Dog Flea Village would be their permanent home, but now they had to flee again. They could now only hope for safety in Rokar Village.

CHAPTER 6

....

ESCAPE TO ROKAR VILLAGE

January 1976

Late that same night, Chamron and his family arrived in Rokar Village. The eleven relatives were tired but thought they had escaped to a safe haven. Crowding into the small shelter, they dropped their bags, lay down, and immediately fell asleep.

They awoke in the morning refreshed and hugged one another in a jubilant family reunion. They believed the threat of death was over. They sat and listened as Nareth and Noe shared what had happened during the eight months of separation.

Nareth explained that he had traveled with his girlfriend's family to Rokar Village. Her parents registered them as a married couple to prevent their daughter from being taken and used by the Khmer Rouge soldiers. Nareth never married her, because her parents did not approve of their relationship. They wanted their daughter to marry a rich man. Nareth was expected to only pretend to be her husband. Her parents did not permit them to sleep together as husband and wife.

Nareth worked long hours in the fields doing rigorous manual labor, yet he was not treated like a respected relative. He prayed for wisdom on how to handle his miserable circumstances, but all too soon, another dangerous situation developed.

Nareth told his girlfriend, "The Khmer Rouge soldiers are patrolling at night. They are looking at the living arrangements of couples registered as married. It is not safe for us to keep sleeping separately."

She rushed to her parents and said, "You must allow Nareth and me to sleep together because the soldiers are spying on us. We will be killed if they realize you lied."

Her parents reluctantly agreed to allow them to live in their house as a married couple.

The family was silent when Narath finished his story. After a few minutes, Noe began to tell his story.

He and his girlfriend, Sokhorn, married when they reached Rokar Village. Her parents objected to their marriage because Noe was not a wealthy man, but the newlyweds were joyful as they made plans to start a family. Tragically, Sokhorn's malnourishment stopped her milk production for their firstborn. The baby died in infancy, and they never had any other children.

One day, when Noe returned from work, a neighbor ran to him and exclaimed, "I saw a group of Khmer

Rouge soldiers drag Sokhorn down to the river. They threw her into a boat and sailed away."

Stunned by this news, he asked, "Where did they take her?"

The neighbor told him he didn't know.

Noe was devastated. He never saw his dear wife again.

After Chamron heard Nareth and Noe's tragic stories, he reached out to comfort them. "Noe, I am sorry you lost your wife and baby. But at last we are together. We can help one another like we did in French Village. I think we should retrieve some of our belongings from Dog Flea Village."

Nareth, Nara, and Chamron snuck back into Dog Flea Village that night. They crept into the east end of the village where Chamron's grandmother's ex-husband, Sarin, lived. Chamron knew God was watching over them, but he had no idea they were heading into danger.

Before they could reach their own shelter, they ran into friends from French Village. These friends told them, "You must not come into Dog Flea Village. Last night Mr. Rouy held a meeting. He announced you and your family are enemies of the government and you will be killed on sight." After hearing this alarming news, they rushed back to Rokar Village without recovering anything from their old shelter.

Chamron's family busied themselves during the January harvest time with usual daily routines. They built their own shelter, had rice, and planted a family garden. Families shared different seeds they had carried with them during their escape. The seeds grew well in the rich soil near their shelters. They had good crops of sweet potatoes, tomatoes, onions, lettuce, corn, peppers, and sugar cane. They harvested nutritious wild morning glory flowers, leaves, and vines from the rice fields to chop up in their soups.

The Communists reminded them that all possessions, including food, belong to the government. The villagers had to be sneaky and steal their own garden produce at night. Any leftover food at the end of the day had to be hidden in their pockets. Salted fish hanging outside to dry had to be concealed in trees. Starvation drove people to steal from one another. Chamron's family stole food from the government, but not from their neighbors.

Their slightly improved life was not to last. Soon, county leaders interrupted the calmness in Rokar Village with a new labor project. They gathered the young frontline group and said, "Pack your clothing, a towel, and a blanket into your backpacks. Get all the village fishing supplies."

Chamron, Nara, and other villagers were forced to walk with the leaders to Norear Village by the Sangker River—a ten-kilometer journey. The group stayed overnight in an old Buddhist temple that was no longer in use.

Pointing to a row of boats, the leaders yelled at the group. "Take these axes, knives, nets, baskets, and buckets and get in the boats." The boats ferried them along the Sangker River to Rangtabal Village. After a half day of travel, they disembarked onto the shore, far from Rokar Village. They unloaded the boats and looked around at the crowds of people from other villages.

"Get busy and build shelters for yourselves," commanded the leaders. "Walk into the forest and collect tree trunks, vines, and branches."

Chamron looked at Nara and said, "Get your ax and knife. We have to follow this order. It is late and will be dark before we get back."

"I just want to rest now," Nara said. "I have no strength to go on."

Chamron encouraged his brother, "We'll do this together. It will be good to have our own shelter."

They toiled building shelters in the 104-degree heat and high humidity. The sweaty laborers worked so closely that their perspiration dripped on one another. The stench of body odor made them cough when they breathed. The red clay-like mud caked on their arms and legs, making them hotter. Bugs clung to the dirt and bit them. No one was allowed to bathe; the smells intensified daily.

After a month of back-breaking labor, the shelters were completed. Now they enjoyed good sleep in their personal quarters. Ten days later, they were startled out of sleep by a loud whistle followed by a soldier screaming orders. "Pack your belongings. We are moving deeper into the forest by the lake."

Chamron, Nara, and the other villagers slowly realized they could no longer enjoy their new shelters by the river. They marched three kilometers through the forest to the lake.

"Stop here," yelled the Khmer Rouge leader. "Set up camp."

They struggled in the darkness to gather wood to build a fire. It was too late to cook, but they needed the protection of the fire to scare away wild animals. The forest was full of snakes, monkeys, and wolves.

At daylight, the villagers assembled by the lake.

"More temporary shelters must be built here," announced the soldiers. They held guns, ready to enforce the order.

Completing a job efficiently or quickly did not bring rewarding compensation, such as rest or a good meal. Instead they faced one tough task after another, week after week. Dreams of sharing a meal with their families—now so far away—filled their minds. Mealtimes were short and the food unpleasant—the same small portions of gruel every day.

After building additional shelters, they were assigned an even more difficult project. The Communist leaders devised a labor-intensive way to remove all the fish from the lake. Traditional fishing equipment and nets would not capture all the fish. The elaborate process started with the creation of a separate pond to temporarily store the fish until they could be transported to Rangtabal Village.

Chamron joined his weak, struggling fellow prisoners in digging a hole fifty meters from the lake. About forty men lined up and passed buckets of water from the lake to the new pond. A whole day of this tedious motion gave them painful shoulders.

It took a week to build a meter-high temporary dike around the lake. Tree trunks, branches, grass, and dirt were hauled to the edge of the lake. The men used short branches to hammer thicker branches into the hard, dry ground to form a trench around the lake. Grass, dirt, and vines were then pounded into the trench to form a strong dike.

The fish in the lakes had to be exposed in shallow water in order to be moved to the pond. The daunting task of reducing the water level in the lake took thirty agonizing days. They tied three long branches with vines to form a tripod. Branches formed long handles which were attached to buckets to swing from the tripods. This apparatus could reach the bottom of the lake and scoop out the water. Six of these tall structures were placed around the lake. Brigades of five men were stationed by the tripods to take turns operating the heavy, swinging buckets. The men scooped out the lake water with this long-handled bucket and dumped it on the ground beyond the sides of the lake. The dike prevented the water from flowing back into the lake. Their arms and backs ached from the repeated motion. The sun burned their skin and insects tormented them as they worked ten hours a day. A group of men patrolled the lake perimeter to assure the dike did not develop holes.

The cook group gathered firewood and small plants for their meals. The workers labored while the soldiers watched. The soldiers allowed them to trap fish in bamboo cages to add to the watery soup. Soldiers took the heartiest portions of food for themselves. The remaining food was only enough to keep the prisoners alive; it was not sufficient to make them strong and healthy.

Once most of the water had been removed, the men were able to begin capturing the fish. Chamron watched the abundant fish swimming in the shallows and wished it was food for his family. Worn out and disillusioned, the men walked into the lake and captured all the fish. The small ones went into the manmade pond while the big ones were sent off to be salted. Completion of moving all the fish did not bring joy—or even relief. No one gave them a good meal or an afternoon to rest. Every minute was work, work, and more work.

They strung the big fish on tree vines by their tails and carried the bulky vines to Rangtabal River. Then, the exhausted workers set up stations to preserve the large fish by salting and smoking them. It took over two months to complete the fishing project near Rangtabal Village.

Chamron was astonished when he found this entire process had to be repeated at two other small lakes in the forest. For two more months, no one had rice, but they had fish. Nearby villagers gave them small amounts of other foods in exchange for fish.

One day, while gathering wood for cooking, Chamron looked up and spied a beehive, as large as an elephant's ear, hanging in the tree branches. He called to his friends. "Come here. I know how we can get this hive. I am going to make a fire."

Taking a flint stone from his pocket, Chamron struck it against a rock to light some tinder and built a fire under the tree. Soon, smoke rose and filled the air, and the bees flew out of the hive. The smoke protected the men from the dazed and angry bees. Chamron climbed the tree and snatched the enormous honeycomb. He tossed it to the men below.

The men cheered in celebration. "We will have sugar for weeks!"

There was enough honey to share among the men. The reward of sweet honey made their boring meals more tolerable and lifted their spirits for a brief time.

At the end of May 1976, Khmer Rouge soldiers forced them to work on a new fishing project. Chamron's group moved to Kampong Prahok Village in Battambang Province near Tonle Sap Lake.

Chamron and a friend boarded a small boat and began a ten-hour day of fishing. Each boat held two fishermen. Everyone worked three shifts—morning, afternoon, and evening. Between shifts, they returned to shore with the catch, and were allowed to eat a portion of fish. They gobbled up the hearty fish and vegetable porridge.

Tonle Sap Lake provided them with more than fish. Using bamboo cages that were two meters long, they trapped fish, snakes, frogs, crabs, and turtles. They hid as much food as possible to take to their shelters at the end of the day. Workdays were too long to allow for propaganda meetings. Chamron gave thanks for that!

At the end of each day, the fishermen transferred their catch from the twenty-five small boats into big boats. The crews on the big boats discarded the heads and tails of the fish. Only the fish bodies were tossed into enormous cement jars full of a preservative salt solution.

One day, when the jars were filled to the top, Chamron's boat pulled alongside the big boat. By accident, his fishing partner stepped on the side of the big boat. The boat tipped and emptied the jar full of salted fish into the lake. The soldiers threatened them with angry voices.

"Why did you do this? You destroyed the catch. We will kill you."

The two froze in fear.

The soldiers pointed their AK-47s at the twenty-five boats. "You must bring back all those fish."

The salted fish parts had sunk three meters to the bottom of the lake.

The fifty fishermen glared at Chamron and his partner, but obeyed, knowing that arguing would produce more trouble.

Everyone jumped into the murky water and dove deep in search of the lost fish. Piece by piece they retrieved fish parts. After hours in the water, their eyes burned red. The repeated dives drained their already weakened bodies. By evening, the jar was only half full.

Miraculously, the Khmer Rouge soldiers' rage diminished. They ordered the men to stop and return to camp. Dog-tired, they shuffled back to camp. No one talked about the horrible day nor mentioned the loss of fish.

A Khmer Rouge soldier noticed Chamron was trustworthy and hard working. He selected Chamron to assist him on a boat ride across Tonle Sap Lake. In the middle of the lake, the engine stalled and made loud noises. The soldier's kind attitude quickly changed. "Turn that knob to the left," he shouted at Chamron.

In his panic, Chamron made a mistake and turned the knob to the right, causing the engine to shut down. Visibly irritated the soldier yelled, "Why did you do that? We could be killed here in the middle of the lake. The storm can sink our boat."

The word *kill* terrified Chamron. The Communist flag was red. That red represented blood and killing to Chamron. The soldiers' eyes looked red to him. He had heard Khmer Rouge soldiers ate human flesh and organs and drank human blood. Soldiers often boasted about their strength increasing after eating human livers. They took pleasure in removing the livers from their live captives and drinking the bile. Chamron shivered. These conversations repulsed him and made him sick to his stomach. It was like tigers devouring their prey.

By this time, Chamron had witnessed many horrific atrocities. He learned to close his mind and heart in order to survive. He protected himself by shutting not his eyes, but his brain. He tried not to think about the alarming events. To take his thoughts to a safe place, he repeated these words from the 23rd Psalm: *Even though I walk through the valley of the shadow of death, I shall fear no evil, for you are with me.* This Bible verse encouraged and strengthened him.

Chamron managed to start the boat and get them to the far side of the lake. He sighed with relief when the soldier disembarked to do his business on shore. Left alone, Chamron sat in the boat thinking about his lack of control over his daily life. He was always obedient and tried to keep a low profile. Still, he was aware he could be killed at any time, for any reason . . . or for no reason at all.

CHAPTER 7

....

SURROUNDED BY DEATH

June 1976

By the end of May all fishing projects were completed. Chamron and Nara reunited with their family in Rokar Village and experienced a few days of rest. Chamron was happy to be with his family on May 31—his nineteenth birthday.

"Grandma, where is Noe?" Chamron asked.

Grandma Rang replied, "Noe disappeared soon after you left. We believe the Khmer Rouge discovered he was a student commando. We have not heard from him in six months. I think they captured and killed him."

This news overwhelmed Chamron and Nara. They looked at each other in shock and disbelief. It was hard to imagine they would never see Noe again.

The rice planting season began in late May and continued into August. They had no rice during this waiting period. Rice would be ready for harvest in

November. In the meantime, they scraped by on soup made of hot water and vegetable leaves. Chamron's family—now a family of ten—consumed all the food they had grown. Lack of sugar, salt, and a proper diet caused their malnourished bodies to swell.

Prakab and Nara traveled from Rokar Village to Tahen Village to visit their friend, Mr. Mui, because they heard he made sugar from palm juice. Once they explained their desperate situation, Mr. Mui felt compassion and gave them sugar and other food supplies. Though they had no control over their dire circumstances, every person in Chamron's family made an effort to acquire food for the group. The Communists had abundant food provisions but behaved as if blind to the suffering all around them. Sharing was out of the question.

Starvation led to many deaths in Chamron's family and throughout Cambodia. Sambath, his seven-year-old brother, fainted while waiting for Narith to serve him some boiled vegetable leaves. His body was swollen; his eyes were white; he never regained consciousness. Seeing Sambath slip from sleep into death broke Chamron's heart.

The siblings wrapped Sambath's body in an old mat. The six remaining brothers carried him to a low hill above the rice field. There was no casket. Weeping, they dug into the hard ground about one foot and put his tiny body in the shallow pit. There was not enough dirt to completely cover him. Chamron and his brothers sat by the grave and mourned for hours.

The next morning, Grandma Rang asked Chamron to fetch his grandfather for breakfast. He shook his Grandpa Nguon and called out, "Grandpa, wake up. It's time for breakfast." When he got no response, Chamron turned him over on the mat and gasped when he saw his dear grandfather had died during the night. Swelling from malnourishment had distorted his body into an elephant shape.

When they first arrived at Rokar Village, two of Chamron's siblings, Pratna and Kosal, were taken away by Khmer Rouge soldiers. They were put in a group with other children and subjected to daily brainwashing. They were systematically taught to obey Angkar.

Kosal was fourteen when he was taken, but bravely managed to escape and rejoin his family in Rokar Village. When he returned, he struggled to explain his escape and what had happened to his sister, a shy ten-year-old girl who had weakened from months of malnourishment.

"Pratna got sick," he told them. "Her skin was hot and sweaty. They gave me permission to take her to a clinic. I saw them give her a shot of something from a Coca-Cola bottle. Her body shook with pain. I held her hand and cried for help, but I couldn't save her. I left the clinic and ran here."

As the family mourned each of their loved one's deaths, others continued to die. Nieces, nephews, and cousins perished from starvation. The village was eerily quiet. So many people were dead or dying.

Chamron was overwhelmed with grief. Death surrounded him. He wondered if he would be next. If he was foolish to dream of having peace and a good life again.

Chamron's Catholic upbringing had not taught him about death. The rules and talk about purgatory confused him. He knew nothing about heaven or what happens after someone dies.

In middle school a missionary gave him an illustrated story of Daniel. He read it as a secular story, not realizing it was from the Bible. In high school, the Gideons gave him a New Testament. He read all twenty-seven books in that Bible. After reading it, he remembered one particular verse—Matthew 10:28: *Do not be afraid of those who kill the body but cannot kill the soul. Rather, be afraid of the one who can destroy both soul and body in hell.* God gave him these words of encouragement from Matthew to liberate him and prepare him for what he would face in the Killing Fields.

All his life, Chamron lived in fear. As a child, he was afraid of the dark, of being alone, of strange music, cemeteries, people wearing camouflage, and bearded men. Whenever he walked alone, he trembled and sang to keep dangers away. But this verse from Matthew changed him from a man gripped with fear to a free man.

By June, Chamron was so weak from starvation, he could no longer work. Unable to move normally, he used a crutch and hobbled and hopped out of the shelter. His body was swollen and shriveled like a popped balloon. Sitting hurt his bottom because so little flesh covered his bones. Leaning on his crutch, he begged in Rokar Village. Many of the families who grew food to use and trade showed compassion to Chamron, giving him small amounts of rice, sweet potato leaves, sugar cane, and green spicy peppers.

After a while, his parched skin stuck to his bones and he was unable to walk at all. Instead he had to crawl from place to place. A fall would break his fragile bones and lead to death. He felt hopeless. He lay on his back on a thin mat and looked at the sky through holes in the hay roof. The holes allowed streaks of sunlight to shine on him. He felt only God could save him.

"Save me, Jesus," he moaned, then shut his eyes and lost the will to live. He wanted to join his grandpa in death. In his despair, Chamron's thoughts turned to God. He remembered the beautiful sound of the Catholic church bell ringing three times a day in French Village. The bell had a heavy, long rope that he would pull to remind the villagers it was time to pray. Not many Catholics stopped to pray, but his family worshiped God three times a day.

Their prayer time in the morning was short because they were busy. At lunch, the prayer time was a little longer. In the evening, they enjoyed a lengthy prayer and praise time. Sitting before an altar with statues of Mary and Jesus surrounded by candles and flowers, his dad would lead the family in prayer. Later, when he was alone, his father used the rosary for further prayer and reflection.

His father was a humble man. He told his family, "I do not have any possessions for your inheritance. All I have to pass on to you is my example of how to love and serve God."

As Chamron lay preparing for death, he fell into a deep sleep. The next morning, he was awakened by loud shouting. Nara and Prakab rushed into the shelter, "Good news! Good news! Mr. Mui has received permission to sponsor our family. We can live with him in Tahen Village. If we stay here, we will die of starvation. They have food there. Hurry! We must leave now."

The news infused Chamron with the strength to stand. He grabbed his backpack and crutch and hobbled outside.

He knew now that God had heard his cries. Packing to leave was slow, because everyone was frail. Carrying even their meager belongings was burdensome. But the prospect of joining Mr. Mui's family gave them hope.

When they reached Tahen Village that night, Mr. Mui welcomed Chamron's family of seven into his shelter. Grandma Rang, Nara, Narith, Prakab, Kosal, Sokha, and Chamron huddled together and fell into a deep sleep.

CHAPTER 8

....

FAMILY FORCED INTO LABOR PROJECTS

July 1976

Mr. Mui made it his first priority to restore the health of the frail group now crowded into his shelter. With big-hearted enthusiasm, he fed the family nutritious foods and palm juice—a source of healthy sustenance. Village leaders had assigned Mr. Mui and his wife, Sakhan, the job of making sugar for the whole village. Palm juice is used to make herbal medicines and sweet desserts. Gathering juice from the palm trees was labor intensive. Working alone, Mr. Mui climbed palm trees to cut the small flowers, which then released juice into bamboo containers.

"I want to train Prakab to work with me collecting the palm juice," he asked a village leader once he was healthy enough to work. "With his help, I can produce more sugar for the villagers."

"You have permission for him to assist you," the leader responded. "Now get back to work."

Mr. Mui instructed Prakab saying, "We must hang all of these cylinders in the palm trees before dark."

Mr. Mui and Prakab strapped bamboo cylinders to their waists. They leaned bamboo branches against the palm trees like ladders. Once at the treetop, they would lift each bundle of flowers and cut them to discharge the sweet juice. They put the cut flower bundles into a cylinder and tied the cylinder to the flower stem. Overnight, the cylinders collected the juice, drop by drop.

Early the next morning, Mr. Mui called to Prakab, "Wake up. We must collect the bamboo cylinders from the palm trees and replace them with clean, empty cylinders. Sakhan will be waiting for the cylinders full of juice."

While Prakab and Mr. Mui worked, Sakhan built a fire under a metal kettle. Then they delivered the full cylinders, and she emptied the palm juice into the kettle. It took three hours for the heat to turn the juice into sugar. Once ready, Sakhan removed the kettle from the fire and stirred the sugar in the pot while it cooled.

She called to Prakab, "The sugar is cool and ready for storage. Bring the clay jars and help me fill them." This preserved sugar would be shared with the whole village.

Under Mr. Mui's watchful eye, each member of Chamron's family regained strength and escaped death.

The family took pleasure in this time of restored health. They attempted to resume their normal day to day lifestyle. But it was not to be.

The Khmer Rouge Communist leaders noticed their recovery and once again disrupted their lives. The siblings were separated and put in different youth groups. Brainwashing started immediately. Systematically, the Communist government broke family ties and demanded total allegiance. All freedoms were stripped away. Villagers had no choice but to obey and follow a set of mind-numbing rules.

Nara and Prakab worked in the rice fields. Chamron was skinny and weaker than the others. Mr. Phan, a Khmer Rouge soldier, was a kind man who received permission for Chamron to work at his house. Good food and time for rest eventually restored Chamron's strength. Soon he was able to care for Mr. Phan's two oxen. As time went on, he watered the garden and helped Mr. Phan's mother plant tobacco. He was thankful to be in this place.

Later, Mr. Phan taught Chamron how to make fertilizer. This product was essential to the farmers, but making it was a dirty, smelly job. Mr. Phan took Chamron to a storage area and told him, "It is your responsibility to gather the materials needed to make fertilizer. Can you see how we have four separate piles, one for each item?"

"Yes," Chamron answered, choking from the ghastly smell.

"Take that wheelbarrow. The old man by the stable will show you where to go first," explained Mr. Phan.

Chamron did as he was told, and when he approached the stable, the old man smiled and handed him a shovel. "Go inside and collect the stool from this cattle stable. Next, get the human waste from each of the village pits."

Every day Chamron repeated this collection process at the village's pits and stables. Even with a shovel, his hands and arms would be covered with waste. He washed himself many times a day but could not wash away the stench.

The animal and human waste formed two of the piles in the storage shed. The third pile was dry leaves from bushes. In the early morning, Chamron gathered the last item—wet leaves from the river. He appreciated the opportunity to go into the cold water. While in the river, he'd search for crabs, frogs, snakes, and fish to put in his waistband to be shared and eaten later.

Next, Chamron used a wheelbarrow to transfer material from each of the four piles and mixed it on the ground to make fertilizer. Other workers transported the fertilizer in oxen carts to the rice fields. Chamron was humbled by this assignment. The work was backbreaking and left him feeling dirty all the time. But he did not grumble nor complain. He had no doubt God had saved him and was responsible for keeping him alive.

Chamron's memories of his childhood connections with God strengthened him during these days of extreme hardship. He remembered how his father would sing the Shepherd's song—the 23rd Psalm—to his family when they assembled outside at the end of the day. That song continued to comfort Chamron when he was weary and smelled of fertilizer.

He had received spiritual guidance from regular worship at the Catholic church on Sundays. His family wore their nicest clothes on that day and sat together in one long pew. The services were from nine to eleven. When he got older, Chamron sang in the choir and served as an altar boy. This was a pleasing ritual, but he had not developed a personal relationship with Jesus.

Completing the fertilizer project brought relief to Chamron. At last, he was far from the foul-smelling storeroom. Next, he planted and cared for corn and sweet potatoes. While waiting for the crops to grow, Tahen Village experienced food shortage and had no rice.

Once in a while, Mr. Phan allowed Chamron to visit his family living in the shelter near Mr. Mui. Another day, he visited Prakab and Nara in the frontline youth camp located in a rice field far from Tahen Village. His brothers told him they were given two canteens of rice porridge twice a day. The thin porridge was made with muddy water and looked like coffee milk, but it was available daily.

Chamron returned to Mr. Phan's home and asked, "May I leave here and join my brothers at the youth camp? I want to be with my siblings."

Mr. Phan reacted with compassion, "Are you sure you want to do that? You are safe here and soon we will have a rich harvest."

"I appreciate all you have done for me," Chamron told him. "Thank you, but I need to be with my brothers."

Leaving Mr. Phan's home turned out to be a bad decision for Chamron. Nara had not explained to Chamron the details of the hard work and harsh living conditions. The youth group lived in temporary shelters with rooftops made of coconut leaves with no sides. Though exhausted, the entire unit had difficulty sleeping. Rain interrupted their sleep. Night after night Chamron lay in wet clothes on a damp mat. Trapped in misery, he regretted having left Mr. Phan's home.

In Cambodia, farmers plant rice from May to August. They plow the ground, sow seeds, and establish irrigation paths to collect rain. The 1976 rice planting season took Chamron even farther from Tahen Village to Kach Rotes Village. This youth camp was by the highway, and its parched land had never been cultivated. The sun beat down on their backs as the young men struggled to break up the dirt clumps in the dry ground.

Rice seeds soaked in water for two nights until tiny roots sprouted. The rooted seeds were sown in the prepared field. It took forty-five days for the rice plants to grow big enough to be bundled. Then they'd be moved to a second, larger field to continue their growth cycle with adequate space.

In July, farmers pulled the rice plants from the fields that had been planted in May. Bundles of wet plants were then tied with long grass. They'd count out eighty bundles of rice plants and trim the tops to make them grow faster once replanted. The saturated bunches were heavy, but the Communists made sure each person carried the maximum number of bundles. Chamron had to carry eighty plants at a time. He'd attach the bundles to his bamboo pole, then walk four kilometers along a crooked and narrow path to an open planting field. Then he'd plant the bundles one-half meter apart. He was thankful for the monsoon season, because once placed in the field, the new plants needed extensive watering.

After weeks of laborious bending and planting, Chamron's knees swelled and he developed a fever. He could no longer walk. Permission for him to return to Tahen Village was denied. His food allowance was reduced, because they decided sick people do not eat much. In this weakened condition, he remained in the youth camp shelter day after day for a month. Nara brought him small portions of food each evening.

One day during Chamron's illness, county leaders visited the camp. He spotted his friend Sean from Dog Flea Village escorting the leaders. Sean entered the camp and Chamron gathered all his strength and called out, "Dear friend, please help me. I need to go to the hospital. They won't let me leave. If I stay here, I'll die."

Sean turned to the county leaders and said, "This man needs to go to the hospital in Tahen Village. May I have permission to make arrangements for him?"

One of the leaders answered him. "Yes, but do it quickly. We must get on with our business."

Sean rushed to his friend's side. He called two men over and told them, "Put this man in your oxen cart and carry him to the clinic in Tahen Village."

The men took him to a clinic in Tahen Village and left him on the dirt floor. Chamron waited in pain for someone to notice him amid the crowds crying for help. A young girl wearing a blood-stained dress saw his swollen legs and helped him to the one empty bed in the corner of the room. No one in his family ever knew he was hospitalized. He never had visitors. But Chamron felt God had sent Sean to save him from death once again.

CHAPTER 9

....

WORKING OUTSIDE TAHEN
VILLAGE

August 1976

After a month of not walking, Chamron's swollen legs recovered. He was able to stand and walk. At the end of August, Chamron was released from the clinic. His request to visit his family was denied. He was not allowed to return home to Grandma Rang, Narin, and Narith. He had to return to work and live with a group of young men in a camp near Tahen Village. They walked five kilometers outside the village daily to plant rice.

Toward the end of one workday, twenty carts full of corn passed by the group. Chamron watched them move along and was surprised to see his friend, Mr. Phan, in the last cart. Two dozen young laborers rushed forward and stole corn from the carts.

Moving away from the crowd, Chamron waited to speak to his friend. "Hello, Mr. Phan. It is good to see you again."

"I am glad you are alive and well," Mr. Phan replied. He tossed Chamron many ears of corn.

Chamron wrapped the corn in his old towel and said, "Thank you so much. This will make a fine meal for me." That evening he cooked some of the corn over a fire—saving the remaining ears for later.

The corn theft was reported, and the group of men was arrested. A guard saw Chamron cooking corn and accused him of stealing. There was no opportunity to explain where he had gotten the corn. Besides, no one would have believed that someone gave it to him.

Six angry Communist leaders surrounded Chamron and the thieves. Other youths at the camp watched as the strong, healthy men pounded the twenty-four skinny men. For over an hour, the enraged leaders punched and kicked the men, even after they fell helpless into the mud. Moaning in pain, they lay on the ground, unable to resist. This was the first time Chamron experienced beating and torture.

When it was over, Chamron lay in the mud and grabbed his chest with both arms and coughed. His breathing was labored. The other youths felt sorry for him as they carried him to his shelter. He could not lie flat, so they put him in a hammock. It was impossible for him to sleep; something was wrong inside his body.

He did not talk. He put all his energy into trying to survive.

After the beating, he could not walk normally. When he tried, he could only hobble one or two steps at a time. He fell and was taken to a clinic in a little house near the camp. Hundreds of people were dropped off by their families and left on the dirt floor next to dead bodies. Chamron thrashed around on a filthy mat with chest and back pain. His body and his bedding were never cleaned. He was surrounded by other smelly patients who moaned in agony. Mold and mildew growing in the cracks of the bamboo walls gave off a rotten odor.

Young, untrained girls gave him ancient herbal medicines. The Khmer Rouge leaders forbade the use of modern medicines, even when they were available. Every day he had severe pain and difficulty walking. Although he never improved, after three months, Chamron was discharged from the hospital.

The leaders did not force him to work because they saw he was too sick. They told him to walk home to Tahen Village. No one followed him nor offered any help. Inner strength alone kept him moving. He knew that if he fell, he would be left to die.

The five-kilometer walk took him the whole day because of his weakened condition. Once he made it home, his grandmother and sisters cared for him. Chamron was crippled and struggled to breathe.

Infected blisters covered his fingers. He punctured the blisters with thorns and soaked his fingers in boiled water full of sour tamarind leaves. The blisters slowly healed, but the rest of his body did not get better over the next two months.

Immobile and feeling miserable, Chamron recalled a conversation he had with his friend Mr. Sang. They'd worked in the youth group—called the front force—together. One day, while working side by side, he told Chamron that his eighty-five-year-old grandmother Sorin had a gift for healing people using massage. He decided this woman would heal him, so he set out to find her. He left his shelter without telling anyone what he planned to do. After nearly two hours, he managed to limp the one kilometer to Grandma Sorin's shelter.

When he was about twenty feet from her, Grandma Sorin saw him and called out, "Come to me, grandchild." He crawled into her shelter and lay on a bamboo mat. Soon, he managed to mumble an explanation. "Communist leaders tortured me and left me to die. A friend took me to a clinic, but my health never got better. They made me leave. I can't eat, breathe, or walk."

"Do not be afraid," she said as she grabbed his arms. "I can help you. You will live and be able to eat and walk home straight."

He was surprised this old woman had enough strength to massage his entire body—hands, fingers, toes, stomach, etc. She pushed, pulled, kneaded, and rubbed him for over an hour.

"Get up, child," she said. "Your body is healed."

Chamron stood. Immediately, he knew she had saved his life with her healing hands. As far as he was concerned, she was a messenger from heaven. He'd again experienced God's awesome grace through this miracle.

Filled with gladness, Chamron sang as he hiked home. He showed his thankfulness by taking Grandma Sorin food whenever he had enough to share.

This miracle left Chamron feeling grateful to God. Before this healing, he never imagined that he would ever again move like a normal person. But now, not only his health but also his joy had been restored. He sang the 23rd Psalm as he walked along.

Grandma Rang, Narin, and Narith could not believe their eyes when they saw him approaching their shelter. Grandma Rang rushed to his side. "Where have you been? We have been looking for you all day."

"How is it you are able to walk?" Narin asked.

Chamron smiled. "It's hard for me to explain. I experienced a miracle."

"How is that possible?" Grandma Rang asked.

"For two hours I struggled to walk to Grandma Sorin's shelter," Chamron answered. "Every part of my body hurt. Grandma Sorin massaged my entire body while I lay on a mat. I sat up and was stunned when she told me to stand up. It was amazing. I could stand without pain. Now I can walk normally."

"This makes no sense," Narith said. "No doctor could help you. Medicines gave you no relief."

"God answered my prayers to be healed," Chamron said. "He made me remember my conversation with Mr. Sang a few months ago. He led me to Grandma Sorin and used her to heal me."

Not long after that healing miracle, Chamron once more experienced diarrhea—worse than ever before. Up to twenty times a day he rushed to the back of his shelter where he had dug a deep hole. The urgency made it impossible to get to a toilet. His sick body carried a disgusting odor from his bowel accidents. He had a fever and experienced nausea and vomiting.

Narith was convinced Chamron was going to die. She decided to take him to Anlongville Hospital. They trudged six kilometers up and down hills in the rice fields. Chamron's foot got caught in the thick grass and he rolled ten meters down a hill. Narith picked up his frail body and carried him on her shoulders the rest of the way to the hospital.

Narith had never been to Anlongville Hospital before. Chamron knew she'd expected to find an orderly, sanitary place with clean bedding and modern medicines. But what they found instead were hallways and rooms covered with blood stains and flies.

They walked around people lying on the dirt floor moaning and crying. Narith spoke to a young girl they found tending to patients. "My brother has had abdominal pain and diarrhea for several weeks. Please take good care of him." She handed the girl a small bag with a clean shirt and pants. Narith wanted to stay with Chamron, but she had to go back to work in the fields. Her group leaders would be looking for her. She would be punished if they discovered her absence.

The girl took Chamron by his arm and led him to an area outside lined with water jars. "Take off your soiled clothing and sit here," she said. Chamron could hear the compassion in her voice. She poured water over his head and all over his body.

The soapy water was soothing to Chamron's sick body. He was embarrassed that he was so dirty and smelly. The girl helped him into his clean clothes, took him back into the hospital and laid him on a small mat. Its linens were soiled and smelled of urine. Restful sleep was not possible, because of the crowds screaming in pain and the family members begging for help. The meager hospital staff was unable to meet the needs of all the patients.

Chamron was hospitalized for seven days. Many patients around him were dying and unable to communicate their needs. Those who did experience healing had to be cautious during personal conversations. The Khmer Rouge soldiers and village spies were everywhere and reported any words of complaint or talk of the past. No one could be friendly and share their story. Anyone caught talking about the past regime would be killed. Not being allowed to connect with others made Chamron feel isolated and lonely, but the week of rest helped him feel better.

The day of his discharge, they gave him sweet and sour soup for lunch. He ate the soup sitting on the mat. He asked for a lemon to make it more flavorful. The sour lemon unsettled his stomach and suddenly cramps interrupted his eating. Chamron did not realize the lemon would trigger the return of diarrhea.

Though unwell, he was forced to leave the hospital. Dehydrated and dizzy, he stumbled along the rugged pathway by himself. About three kilometers into his walk, he spotted a place that made palm juice. Beads of sweat from his fever dripped into his eyes. His dry throat made it hard to swallow. Diarrhea persisted and soiled his clothes. Feeling faint and reeking of foul odors, he fell on a pile of rice plants that had been stacked like hay for the animals. He lay there motionless.

Villagers had noticed him struggling to walk as he approached. They watched him fall to the ground. One of them pointed and said, "Look, another one dying. Let's carry him to the shade and give him palm juice and food."

For a few hours, Chamron rested in the shade of a nearby tree. The juice and food revived him. He looked over at the villagers working in the field and called out, "Thank you for rescuing me. I must get going before dark."

As he stood up, Chamron managed to smile. He realized he'd once again been saved from death.

Walking three kilometers in the oppressive heat soon sapped his remaining energy. He was thirsty and frantic to find water. In Tahen Village, he drew close to some strangers. He called up to them in their shelter and begged, "Please, I need water."

One of the men pointed to a large clay jar and said, "Go see if there is any water there."

The water in the jar was low. His hands were shaking as he grabbed a coconut shell and scooped up some of the bug-filled water. He saw the bugs, but drank the water anyway. He looked up at the men. "Thank you."

His eyes were blurry with fever and his body ached, but he managed to make it home. As soon as Narith saw him on the path near their shelter, she rushed out and put her arms around him and guided him inside. Despite his health problems, he felt at peace in Tahen Village.

Chamron was permitted to recuperate at home for only a few days. He was commanded to rejoin the youth workforce planting rice outside Tahen Village. Chamron, now twenty, was weakened from illnesses and carried fewer rice bundles than required.

On a stormy day in July, he slipped from the narrow, muddy path and collapsed into the water-logged rice field. His bamboo pole fell across his neck. "Help me," he cried. "I can't get up."

No one heard his cries because of the noise of the thunderstorm.

Covered with mud in the pouring rain, a vision of the stained-glass windows in his childhood church came to mind. The windows showed the Stations of the Cross. He envisioned the one showing Jesus falling as he carried the cross. Comforted and strengthened, he pulled himself back onto the path. His fear of death disappeared; God was with him. He picked up the rice bundles and headed to the mucky field.

The rice planting project ended in August and the waiting period for the November harvest began. No one was allowed to rest. Without delay, the Khmer Rouge Communists assigned the young workforce to a new project. In September, Chamron was sent with this group to the frontline special force far from Tahen Village. He was happy to find Nara was in his unit. They were assigned to build miles of canals for an irrigation system. To qualify for meals, they were expected to dig holes three meters deep and two meters wide. They enlisted friends to help if they realized they could not achieve the daily requirement. Failure resulted in punishment and no food. The canals irrigated the rice fields along Highway 4 from Svay Chek Village to Kampong Preah Village—about twenty kilometers east of Battambang City.

At the end of long days spent digging holes deeper than their own height, they fell asleep in abandoned buildings by the road. For months they worked too far away to visit their families in Tahen Village. Chamron missed his family. He risked punishment when he slipped out one night to visit them. He was able to hurry back before his absence was discovered.

Chamron and Nara worked on the canal project for the next three months. In December of 1976 they were sent back to the fields to harvest rice bundles.

Chamron crept away to visit his younger brother Prakab, who was working in a sugar cane field. While they chatted, Chamron poked the ground looking for edible roots. Prakab tossed him five stalks of sugar cane. Chamron took a bite. "Thank you, brother," he said. "This tastes so good. I will take these and eat them later. I must hurry before they realize I am gone."

The pieces of sugar cane were heavy and fell out of his pants. A young guard in the sugar cane field saw him and raised his knife as he yelled, "Stop, thief! I know you stole that sugar cane. I will kill you."

"I am not a thief!" Chamron said. "I was given these pieces of sugar cane. I have a knife too, and I am not afraid to die."

The guard left to report the incident to his leaders.

Chamron was allowed to explain what had happened and was surprised that he evaded punishment. He returned to work clearing and preparing overgrown land for future rice planting.

During the planting season, Chamron and Nara endured hardships of malnourishment, exhaustion, bouts of dysentery, and weakness. These young men of twenty and twenty-one were worn down physically and mentally by the punishing labor.

CHAPTER 10

....

LIFE CONTROLLED BY THE
KHMER ROUGE

August 1977

After the sugar cane incident, Chamron tried to keep a low profile and stay out of trouble. During the summer of 1977, Communist leaders noticed his perseverance and hard work. They rewarded him with a job in the kitchen room. For a few weeks, he got larger portions of food.

The September through October monsoon season inundated the area with flood waters, keeping everything wet all the time. Chamron carried his food rations in a bowl through the swampy terrain from the kitchen to the camp. The water came up to his waist. One night, in his weakness, he stumbled and dropped his food, leaving him nothing to eat.

That night his stomach growled with hunger. Hidden in the darkness, he gathered morning glories from the rice field and climbed a tree to get tamarind fruit. This dark-green fruit was the size of his thumb and had a sour taste like lemons. He satisfied his hunger with the mouthwatering fruits and morning glories and quickly fell asleep. After that stumble and fall, he ate his food rations by the kitchen room.

Hunger haunted Chamron day and night. He searched for something—anything—to eat. He spotted men with dried corn kernels and begged for a cup. He devoured the dried kernels and instantly fell to the ground in pain. Diarrhea again wracked his puny body. Dehydration swiftly stole what little strength he had left. He lay on the ground outside the kitchen room too weak to swat the flies that crawled all over his body.

"Help me," he cried out. "I am dying. Take me to a clinic."

The leaders glanced over. One of them yelled, "It's your fault you are sick. You shouldn't have eaten the corn."

Two of Chamron's friends came over and said they would take him to the clinic. "May we use the oxen cart?" one of them asked the leaders.

"No! You may not use the oxen cart. Get him up and go now."

His two friends lifted him off the ground and carried him over their shoulders. His legs dragged as the three of them slogged through mud to the Buddhist temple in Tahen Village. They were shocked to find that the Buddhist temple and the statues that once surrounded it had been destroyed. Only a few war-torn walls remained. All traces of religion had been wiped out. Monks were dressed in black like everyone else; their colorful orange garments were gone. Now homeless, the monks lived in the streets near the ruined temple structure.

The clinic was set up in the temple ruins and staffed with untrained girls ages twelve to twenty. They escorted Chamron to a mat stained with urine and feces, where he collapsed and fell asleep. His illness was treated with painful shots using dirty syringes and village medicines stored in contaminated Coke bottles. The pills he was given were the ones made by the old people using ancient recipes of roots, honey, and herbs. The kind workers did not report his behavior when he crept out of his room in search of fruits growing around the building.

He was permitted to bathe in the river in front of the temple. Patients liked to gather on the temple steps and rest in the sun. Once, he slipped when weaving through the crowd on the cement steps. He gashed his leg and tumbled to the ground. The severe leg injury became infected.

Day after day, week after week, people all around Chamron died. This three-month stay in the clinic was a time of pain, misery, and sadness. He felt alone, and longed to be in the company of family, where he could talk and receive encouragement. His family lived close by, but they didn't know he'd been hospitalized so he never had any visitors.

Some of the other patients received visitors. They brought food and encouragement for their loved ones. If only he could have had even simple conversations with them as well, but he had to resist. It was impossible to know who was a spy disguised as a patient. These spies would try to trick you into saying something about the past to receive the reward of good favor with village leaders and possible promotion.

There were no trained personnel on site to medically treat any of the illnesses. The unclean conditions in the building spread disease. Chamron recovered from diarrhea and his leg eventually healed, despite not having any medications to fight the infection. However, his body remained weak from insufficient nutrition.

In November 1977, the harvest season began. Chamron was discharged from the clinic and ordered to return to his frontline unit. Instead, he went home. Grandma Rang, who didn't realize he'd been in the clinic for months, was astonished to see him. She celebrated his return by cooking his favorite dish of noodles. Family care, rest, and better food helped restore his strength.

From their shelter, Chamron's family heard the loudspeakers mounted on tall poles along the main road in Tahen Village erupt with an unusual announcement. All villagers were to go to a government meeting in Norea Village. Chamron's family traveled two hours to attend the gathering. They sat in the hot sun in a barren field all day and tried to make sense of the troubling news.

The loudspeakers there delivered a grave declaration: "All of Cambodia is now a Communist country."

Prior to this announcement, the government was never labeled Communist. The Khmer Rouge Communist party controlled Cambodia for years, but they called themselves Angkar.

The day unfolded in the following manner:

- First, formal introduction of Communist leaders, followed by reports on work progress.
- We were challenged to work harder.
- We were given a presentation of a plan to create miles of ponds by damming the river.
- A drama skit featuring brave Khmer Rouge soldiers conquering Republic soldiers was presented to us.
- Finally we were shone a propaganda documentary film detailing the Khmer Rouge Revolution. The footage showed the history of their conquest of Cambodia.

The film reminded Chamron of his former life in French Village, watching movies with his friends. In high school, he loved going to all kinds of movies— Chinese, Cambodian, Kung Fu and action dramas with cowboys—Clint Eastwood, John Wayne, Charles Bronson, and Charlie Chaplin were his favorites.

Battambang City had six movie theaters. A small car with a speaker would drive by the school and through the marketplace advertising the movies for that day.

During the two-hour school recess periods, Chamron watched movies. The ticket price was low for front row seats; the more expensive seats were in the back of the theater. All seats were assigned. He and his friends bought one ticket and sat on one another's laps. His two best friends had more money than he did and always paid for Chamron. In addition, he enjoyed movies on weekend mornings before doing volunteer work at the Catholic church.

Chamron's craving to see movies was so intense that he even watched ones in the Chinese language. He viewed his favorites over and over. In the labor camp, he longed for a quiet escape into a movie theater.

When they returned home from that meeting, Chamron was afraid the Communists would search for him when they discovered him missing from his frontline unit. Consequently, he chose to leave the safety of his home in order to protect his family. If caught sheltering him, they would be punished. He embraced Grandma Rang one more time and left in the cover of darkness.

After walking for hours, he climbed into a tree to rest. He tied himself to branches so he would not fall as he slept. Without thinking, he lit a cigarette. The lighter flashed in the darkness. A Communist soldier passing by saw the flame.

"What are you doing up there? Come down!"

Chamron stayed calm as he explained. "I am trying to make my way back to my work unit on the frontlines. I just got out of the hospital."

Thank goodness they believed him.

He stayed with the patrol group that night. In the morning, he was led to the front lines of the workforce. The work crew gave him a knife to clear out brush and roots. This knife came in handy that evening when he wanted to cook rice in the field.

An old man he'd met on the fish-catching project had taught him how to cook without a pot. Using his knife, Chamron whittled a branch to form a shovel and used it to dig a hole the size of a cooking pot. He lined the hole with leaves and filled it with rice grain he had hidden in his old towel. Covering it with leaves and dirt, he lit a fire over the hole, then relaxed while his rice meal cooked for an hour.

Chamron spent the next months working on the frontline clearing land for rice planting. He was weary and in pain. He couldn't imagine his life could become more unbearable.

One morning in February 1978, he was told to take the oxen to feed on grass near the field pathways. While there, he witnessed a young man stealing rice grain. Soldiers caught the thief, who immediately pointed at Chamron and said, "He stole grain too."

Once again, he was wrongfully accused of theft. The soldiers didn't believe Chamron was caring for the oxen.

With arms bound behind their backs, Chamron and the thief were led back to the village. The Khmer Rouge soldiers roped them to a group of thirty other prisoners. They dragged the men to a company of Communist soldiers and shoved them to their knees. The soldiers grabbed the prisoners' necks and hit each of them twenty times with a bamboo rod as thick as a man's arm. Chamron's hands were bound so tightly that he fell to the ground with each blow and water poured out of his mouth. His body crumpled in pain. He cried out, "Save me, Jesus." It was a miracle that none of his bones were broken.

After the beatings, the prisoners were tied to poles and made to sit outside in the heat with no water or protection from mosquitoes. The person guarding them was from Chamron's village. This guard's father had sold water to Chamron's family. The man could have helped Chamron escape, but he turned away and treated him like a stranger.

That night in Tahen Village, Chamron crouched in pain with the group of prisoners. At daylight, the captors untied them and thrust shovels into their hands. Beaten and hardly able to move, they trudged all day to Roneam Forest. The soldiers led them to a flooded rice field and told them to make a dam. The three meters of water were over their heads. They could not stand up in the deep hole. Chamron and the others dove into the water and shoveled dirt to carry up to form a dam.

Most of the dirt dissolved and disappeared from their hands before they reached the surface. Their eyes burned red from working under the murky water. Mosquitoes covered their wet bodies when they sat on the shore. Even cooking fires did not drive away the mosquitoes. Communist leaders never expected this dam to be built. The task was designed to be torture.

The night air was cold that time of year. Chamron found an old rice sack to crawl into during the night. This sack gave him some warmth and protected him from the mosquitoes.

He spent months in this labor camp. The prisoners had no tools or machinery—all work was done with their bare hands. The job to contain the flood waters by building a dam was never successfully completed. The December monsoon flooded all the fields; planting was impossible in the marshy soil.

No longer bound to a row of prisoners, Chamron was expected to put in a good day's work building dams. Toiling in the flooded fields, he was surprised when he caught sight of his brother Nara kneeling not far from him. He whispered, "Nara, come stay with me tonight."

Nara responded, "Brother, I will try to come."

Every night, the Communists counted the prisoners in the shelters. Nara never went to stay with Chamron. Instead, he escaped from the prison camp and left without telling Chamron. Upon finding Nara missing from the camp, four Communist soldiers pulled Chamron out of his rice sack in the middle of the night. They threw him to the ground, kicked, and beat him. They screamed, "Where is your brother? We know you helped him escape. When we find your brother, we will behead both of you."

Half asleep and confused, Chamron replied, "I don't know where Nara is." Hearing them talk of beheading, Chamron started to create an escape plan of his own. He had to get out of the prison camp in Roneam Forest. He was certain they were going to kill him.

Lighting the way with an oil lamp, one soldier shouted, "Get moving. Lead us to him." Another Communist leader whipped Chamron's hands and body as he staggered in the dark. His failure to find Nara led to more torture. They were furious and decided Chamron was being uncooperative. They pounded his whole body until he was black and blue and bloody. The pain left him numb and unable to scream.

Four leaders grabbed his arms and legs and hurled him into muddy flood waters that surrounded the camp. Figuring he was dead, they stormed away.

Overcome with excruciating pain, he again mumbled the words, "Save me, Jesus." Grabbing stubby grass, he dragged himself out of the water and back onto the shore. There in front of him was his cherished rice sack. Cold and drenched, he wiggled into his sack, but he spent a sleepless night inside, hurting all over and shaking in his wet clothes.

The next morning, he was discovered alive and ordered back to the fields. They demanded he work, even though he stumbled on the pathway and fell over and over again. Late that afternoon, he again prayed, "Save me, Jesus." This time he added, "Blind the eyes of my enemy so I can escape."

He needed to get far away from the prison camp. In clear view of the guards, he staggered one kilometer from the field to Ream Jakrey Village searching for Nara. The guards never caught sight of him passing by.

CHAPTER 11

···

GOD'S RECURRING
PROTECTION

March 1978

As soon as Chamron arrived in Ream Jakrey Village, he saw Grandma Pehn, his neighbor from French Village. He greeted her, then leaned against a wooden bench for support and confided, "I have escaped from the prison camp in Roneam Forest. I can't keep running. I don't know where to go."

Grandma Pehn placed a warm hand on Chamron's arm. "Come with me to my shelter." He followed her to her home, where she fed him fish before instructing him further. "Go find my son Nhep in Chroy Sdao Village. He will provide a safe place for you."

Before beginning the search for Nhep, Chamron slept in the safety of Grandma Pehn's home. When he woke, she gave him a rice pot, a small towel, and a hat.

He knew it would be a two-day walk to Chroy Sdao Village.

Chamron picked the bean-like pods of tamarind fruit from trees in the rice field by Grandma Pehn's home. He ate some of the sweet-sour fruit, then started to throw the rest away, but was puzzled by the words that filled his mind. *Keep the leftover fruit in your rice pot.*

Chamron quickly understood God was talking to him, but he questioned God, saying, "Why should I keep it? Tamarind fruit is abundant in the fields."

He remained motionless and listened as God repeated the command three times. *Keep the fruit in your rice pot.*

Chamron still didn't understand, but concluded he had to be obedient and carry the fruit with him.

He began his walk along the highway toward Chroy Sdao Village. He wanted to find Grandma Pehn's son Nhep as soon as possible. With enemies all around, he did not feel safe walking out in the open.

That evening, he reached Panha Buddhist Temple and found some old friends from French Village. These friends shared some small root pieces of sweet potatoes. He was thankful for their generosity. And though the food helped, he was exhausted from his journey and planned to stay the night under a wooden cart. But before he could fall asleep, loud noises from the highway startled him, and he jumped.

He heard God's voice again: *Go check it out.*

Chamron stretched to ease his stiff and weakened arms. He knew he must get up and move on. Gathering his few belongings, he made his way to the highway, where he found a multitude of people and oxen pulling wooden carts. He asked one of the women, "Where're you folks heading?"

The woman, holding a baby, told him, "We're going to Omany Village."

"May I join you?"

"Yes, come with us."

Chamron felt safer with this band of travelers than walking alone in the dark. Strangely though, there was no further conversation during their journey. The silent group approached the bridge in Anlong Village.

Three Communist guards on the bridge scanned them with flashlights. The brightness shone on Chamron. He looked around. He was stunned to discover he was alone. The crowd had disappeared.

"How is this possible?" he wondered. "I know I didn't imagine all those people walking with me. Has God sent a band of angels to protect me?"

Chamron escaped from the light by leaping off the freeway and hiding out of sight. Before he fled under an old trailer, he tossed his rice pot. It landed next to a tree. He lay motionless and pretended to be asleep.

"Save me, Jesus," he prayed.

Footsteps crunched on the leaves. The guards searched with their flashlights around the area where the rice pot had crashed against the tree trunk. One of them found it and opened it.

"There's fruit in this pot. That man is not trying to escape. He must have come from the rice fields."

If they'd thought he was an escapee, Chamron knew he would have been found and shot. He lay in the darkness pondering how God had saved him from certain death. He now understood His plan. He'd used the fruit to spare him from torture and killing.

"Thank you, Jesus, for giving me another day," he prayed out loud once the guards had left. Then he closed his eyes and enjoyed a peaceful night of sleep at last.

***

The Communist guards slept during the day. At first daylight, Chamron climbed out from under the trailer and crossed the bridge. Checking constantly to be sure no soldiers were in the vicinity, he progressed past Battambang Airport. When he got to his old high school, he recalled crossing the bridge with his brothers when the Khmer Rouge soldiers invaded the city three years before—April 17, 1975. He remembered how they had watched and shook hands with the soldiers while shouting, "Welcome! Welcome!" Now, the people around him were sweeping the littered street with coconut brooms.

A Communist soldier on a bicycle pointed at him. "Where're you going? Why aren't you at work?"

With unexpected confidence, Chamron faced the soldier and told a bold lie. "I'm carrying rice soup to my brother guarding the old bridge."

The soldier waved his gun. "Move along then."

Chamron had intended to cross the railroad bridge at Otambang Village, but soldiers working on the bridge made that route too dangerous. He instead headed south to Sangker River.

As soon as he arrived at the river, a young girl fishing with her father looked at him and said, "Come have breakfast with us." She offered him a bowl of rice and fish.

The words *I shall not want* from the 23rd Psalm came into his mind. God had once again sent two angels to care for him. Tears streamed down his face. He took the bowl. "Thank you for this hearty meal."

After eating, Chamron asked, "Can you take me across the river?"

"Get in my boat," the father replied kindly.

Once across the river, Chamron climbed onto the bank and waved good-bye. He called out, "Thank you for helping me. You blessed me with good food and a safe boat ride."

He journeyed on foot along the riverbanks to the upper market. There he observed boats filled with families. He listened to their chatter and laughter. Loneliness overcame him when he thought about his own family so far away. Fed up with his miserable circumstances, he hung his head as he approached the village kitchen and begged a woman for food. The older woman's eyes looked at him with compassion and fed him a nourishing bowl of vegetables, dried fish, and rice porridge. Chamron gripped the bowl and gobbled the rich porridge.

Despite the woman's good intentions, it proved to be too much too fast. Chamron doubled over in pain minutes later when his shrunken stomach could not cope with the large portion of food. It had been a year since he'd eaten abundantly. Groaning in agony, he clutched his stomach and fell to the ground. He closed his eyes and again cried, "Save me, Jesus."

For several hours, Chamron was unable to stand up or move. Eventually, he rolled over, realizing he had been delayed a long time. Forcing himself to his feet, he pressed on toward Chroy Sdao Village.

By nightfall, he'd managed to get only as far as Phnom Kror Poe—Crocodile Village. He had expended all his energy, and even though his stomach remained sore, he was hungry again. He begged for food at the adult kitchen room. After eating some meager scraps, he collapsed and fell asleep by the kitchen fire pit.

In the middle of the night, two Communist soldiers awakened him with kicks to his back. One of them yelled, "Strangers are not welcomed in this village." They dragged him to the village leader's house.

The leader interrogated him, asking, "Where did you come from? Why are you here? Where are you going?"

Chamron was given no time to respond. He stood in silence with his head down and then dropped to his knees and begged. "Please have mercy on me." He expected to be killed for trying to escape.

"I know you are an escaped prisoner," the village leader said. "You're not free to travel. I should kill you. Tomorrow we will take you back to the prison camp in Roneam Forest where you belong."

The interrogation abruptly ended. Chamron was pushed away from the leader's shelter and shoved to the ground near the kitchen fire. He crouched low and waited for the soldiers to walk away. Then he prayed, "Thank you, God. It's by your mercy that I'm still alive."

CHAPTER 12

....

SAFETY IN SNUNG VILLAGE

March 1978

Feeling sluggish, Chamron slept for a few hours and awoke before sunrise. He knew his only chance of escape was to leave in darkness. He crept away from the kitchen and headed west along the canal to Snung Village.

He managed to keep moving all day—one slow step at a time, hour after hour. It was dark when he stumbled into Snung Village. Starvation forced him to beg one of the kitchen room guards to give him food. After Chamron ate, he was told to leave. The guard seemed to be helpful when he said, "Cross the highway and ask for Mr. Phan. He is the leader of Snung Village."

As soon as Chamron heard the name Mr. Phan, he received a warning from God saying, "Don't go there." He recalled how the Lord used the tamarind fruit in his rice pot to save him by the bridge. He understood he must listen to the Lord and be obedient.

Though exhausted from running and hiding all day, he left Snung Village. He walked only a short distance before flopping down and falling asleep. He was sheltered by some trees near a pond. He awoke refreshed after a few hours of rest.

That morning, he arrived at Chroy Sdao Village and began looking for Grandma Pehn's son, Mr. Nhep. At the kitchen room, he found one of Mr. Nhep's friends and asked, "Can you help me find Mr. Nhep?" A man answered, "I don't know where he is. I haven't seen him today."

Chamron felt finding Mr. Nhep was important to his survival, so he wandered around the village asking one man after another, "Have you seen Mr. Nhep?"

Each time, he got the same response: "I don't know where he is."

He searched all day, but never located Mr. Nhep. He had no idea what to do next. With misgivings and feeling despondent, he decided he should return to Snung Village. But his hunger led him back to the Chroy Sdao kitchen room.

A young boy stood in the path blocking the way. "Uncle, don't go there," he said.

Chamron was tired and hungry. He had no patience with this boy obstructing his way. "Why?" he grumbled. "I'm starving. I must go there. Get out of my way!"

Three times the boy repeated the warning, saying, "Don't go there."

Chamron ignored him, pushed him aside, and walked to the kitchen room. He glanced back at the boy's sad face as he passed him. A female soldier chopping vegetables with her bayonet pointed at Chamron and said, "You're the enemy. I can see from your sweaty body that you escaped from the forest and have been running." In her thunderous voice, she threatened him. "You'll be executed when the chief commander returns."

Chamron could not control the shaking of his frail and skinny body. He glanced back to where the boy had been standing, but he'd disappeared. Chamron should have listened to his warning. He regretted his failure to recognize God's intervention.

The woman's demeanor changed when she noticed how scared and silent he was. She patted his shoulder and changed her accusing tone saying, "Don't be afraid. No one will hurt you. You'll be all right. Stay here. I'll get food for you."

Chamron waited for food, but instead she came back with two Communist soldiers, each carrying a long sword. They grabbed his scrawny arms and dragged him to the commander's house where they flung him to the ground under the building. Two guards sat on either side of him, blocking his escape with their swords.

"Please do not kill me," Chamron begged. "Let me go. I'm not the enemy."

In his heart he cried out, *Save me, Jesus*.

A guard poked him with his sword handle and shouted, "Shut up or I'll kill you now!"

At that very moment, a miracle happened. Ten Communist soldiers rode up on bicycles. The two guards who'd been watching Chamron left and greeted these soldiers. "Welcome, friends. Come inside and visit."

Chamron watched as they climbed up the twenty-five steps to the front door. He patiently waited until all twelve men disappeared into the house. Once inside, they seemed to have completely forgotten about him.

The Lord had again provided an opportunity for Chamron to escape.

His legs were cramped from squatting so long and he struggled to move. Ignoring the pain, Chamron scrambled from under the house and hid in an irrigation ditch. When he felt it was safe, he trekked back to Snung Village to search for Mr. Phan—the leader of Snung Village. He wanted to ask for shelter and a job.

He stood in the middle of the village hoping to find Mr. Phan. A woman from the kitchen room noticed him. Taking pity on him, she filled a plate with food and walked toward him.

The woman asked Chamron, "What's your name? Where're you from?"

"I'm Chamron from Zone Four."

She handed him the food. "Why are you here? Who are you looking for?"

Chamron took the plate. "Thank you for the food. I'm looking for Mr. Phan. Can you help me?"

"Stay put," the kind woman replied, then rushed away.

A few moments later, a man yelled in the distance. Chamron couldn't make out what he was saying, but God told him it was Mr. Phan. After a while, the man approached him.

"Oh, son, you are a lucky man. And do you know why I say you are a lucky man? Because yesterday we were told to kill all escapees. Today you are spared because the government changed the rules."

Instantly Chamron knew. God had shaped the circumstances to involve him in a search for Mr. Nhep—a hunt Chamron thought was a waste of time. But God's perfect timing had saved his life.

Mr. Phan looked warily at Chamron's undernourished body. Certainly he doubted how much use to him Chamron would be.

"What can you do?" he asked Chamron. "Can you chop wood?"

"Yes, I can do that."

Every day for a month, God gave Chamron the strength to chop wood for Mr. Phan. He gathered wood, tended the cooking fire, and slept in the kitchen room on a bamboo mat. He was thankful to have a roof over his head. And in return for his hard work, he was given plenty of good food.

Chamron's body strengthened and his hair grew long like Samson's. He was given additional responsibilities assisting the cook, Ms. Khim. He hauled water, chopped wood, and prepared the kitchen fire for her. She had no sons, but treated him like one and called him Ron. She gave him extra food and showed him love and respect. Thinking about the future, Ms. Khim said, "Ron, when we become a free country again, I want to train you in my craft. I was not always a cook. I made jewelry using gemstones. I want you to be my adopted son."

Chamron thought for a moment, then said, "I am all alone now and I have no plans for my future. I will go with you."

The woman's kindness made Chamron think of his mother. His mother did not read or write, but she was wise in many ways. She was a midwife in their village. Only rich people went to the hospital during pregnancy. He had watched his mother help many women deliver babies in their homes. During labor, he would help by filling a basin with warm water to wash the babies. He remembered his mother's gentleness and love for her family and friends.

In late December, Mr. Phan asked Chamron to leave. "You are no longer weak. You are a strong man now. I want you to quit working in the kitchen and care for my oxen." Mr. Phan allowed him to sleep and eat in the kitchen room, but he no longer worked there.

Chamron respected Mr. Phan and headed to the rice field with the oxen. He benefited from this new job. In the rice fields, he caught fish, crabs, and frogs with his bare hands. It was a delightful change for him. God provided him with rice, sugar cane, and more nutritious food in the rice field.

Chamron recalled the wonderful years of Christmas celebrations with his family. People would make small and large bamboo stars, then cover them with transparent colored paper and lights. The large stars were hung over front doors or on outside gates. The small stars dangled in windows.

Christmas was a joyous time of year. Life-sized figures of Mary, Joseph, and the shepherds and magi were displayed inside the church. The priest sprayed cologne on baby Jesus as people proceeded by the manger. Everyone put money in a big basket placed near baby Jesus.

On Christmas Day, the drama of Jesus' birth was performed. When Chamron was a small boy, he played a sheep. When he was older, he got to be a shepherd. His sisters and brothers sang hymns in the special choir and read Scripture. It was a family time of praise and worship. But now, the Communists had banned all religious activities. No one was allowed to even speak of those past festivities.

Throughout harvest time, Chamron piled up loose hay for the oxen. There was no grass for them during this dry season. In the late afternoon on January 7, 1979, he was leading the oxen back to the village. As he approached, he saw a large group of people creating a commotion with their exuberance. When he was close enough, he heard a voice coming from the radio and then understood their excitement.

"The Khmer Rouge Communist regime has ended," the voice announced. "The North Vietnamese Communists have taken control of Cambodia."

All over the village, Cambodians were celebrating their new freedom with song and dance. Despite the joy he saw, Chamron had a bad feeling. He was afraid to continue herding the oxen toward home. He perceived danger, so he backed off the street and hid behind a tree. From there, he noticed the Khmer Rouge soldiers posted all around the village.

Chamron soon heard shouts announcing the Vietnamese capture of the capital city of Phnom Penh, then watched as heavily armed Khmer Rouge soldiers rode through Snung Village on horseback. From a distance, he listened in horror to screams as the soldiers murdered the celebrating people.

Noise of gunfire filled the air. Chamron ducked to the ground behind a bush. As he waited in hiding, he was reminded of another time he'd heard gunfire, back in middle school. That time, he'd watched soldiers travel by train through his city. Sometimes they'd drop bullets and shells near the train station. Students picked up these bullets and used rocks to blow them up. One of his friends did this on the school steps with disastrous results. Chamron had stood nearby and was traumatized as he watched his friend bleed and die from the resulting explosion. This was the first time he'd witnessed a violent death. Classes were canceled and everyone was sent home. He was horrified by the gruesome memory brought on by the powder charge of these bullets today.

Chamron continued to observe the chaos from his hiding spot. He watched as some villagers headed west in their efforts to escape. The Khmer Rouge soldiers rounded up the frantic group and pushed them east. Cambodians were caught in a war between the Khmer Rouge soldiers and the North Vietnamese soldiers. Some of the Vietnamese soldiers were Cambodian. Chamron later learned that there were two groups that day:

- Group One—The Khmer Rouge Communist army, who had a genocidal plan to kill every villager. They forced villagers to dig pits all over the country to bury the bodies.
- Group Two—The Cambodian soldiers and North Vietnamese Communist soldiers, who fought against the Khmer Rouge troops in an effort to liberate and protect Cambodians.

Seeing carnage all around him, Chamron rushed to leave Snung Village. He had a close relationship with his seventy-year-old adopted stepmom Ms. Khim, and decided to head to Borvel Village with her, her husband, daughter and son-in-law, and grandchild. The six of them, after finding each other in the chaos, left with two oxen pulling a wooden cart. They headed north to escape the battles raging in the village.

On the path, Chamron found a new fishing net about fifty meters long. He put this valuable net into his backpack. He lugged bags of kitchen supplies on each end of the bamboo pole he held across his shoulders. Another bundle full of clothing balanced on his head. By now, he was strong and able to carry the heavy load.

Missiles and rockets flew around them as they rushed out of Snung Village. They heard AK-47 bullets flying by, but no one in his group was harmed. Nothing exploded. Chamron felt God was shielding them from all the weapons.

The North Vietnamese came in tanks and chased away the Khmer Rouge Army. Once Chamron's party heard the liberation announcement, they turned around and headed back to Snung Village.

The genocide finally ended. Cambodians had suffered at the hands of the Khmer Rouge from April 17, 1975 to January 7, 1979. It had been three years, eight months, and twenty days. Chamron's life of hell was over.

Chamron was now twenty-one and deeply grateful to be alive. And there in the midst of the Killing Fields, he'd made a covenant to serve God all the days of his life.

CHAPTER 13

······································

JOY FOLLOWED BY DISILLUSIONMENT

January 1979

On January 7, 1979 the Khmer Rouge Communist regime ended. Families ran from village to village in search of surviving relatives. Some sought revenge, killing the Khmer Rouge who had tortured them and massacred their family members. A search for food consumed the starving villagers. Healthier individuals got to work selling food and produce in the marketplace.

Chamron didn't return to his own family. He chose to remain with Ms. Khim's family in Snung Village. Chamron was a good fisherman. He caught numerous fish in the net he'd found. In this way, he provided food for Ms. Khim's family. He loved Ms. Khim and embraced her as his stepmother. He decided to relocate with her when she wanted to move to Borvel Village.

On the way, they stopped in Tmorkol Village for a few days and rested in an empty college building.

During this stay, Chamron began to wonder about his own family. Were they back in French Village? Had they survived?

Chamron approached Ms. Khim and asked, "May I go to French Village to check on my family?"

"Yes, you may go," Ms. Khim replied.

Chamron hurried off to French Village in hopes of seeing his mom, Grandma Rang, and his siblings—Narin, Narith, Nareth, Nara, Darab, Prakab, Kosal and Sokha. His other three siblings—Noe, Pratna and Sambaht—and sixteen additional relatives had died of starvation or were murdered by the Khmer Rouge Communists.

Chamron walked eagerly all day, anticipating an enjoyable reunion with his family. Grandma Rang was the first person he saw when he walked into their shelter. Shock lit up her face when she saw him.

"Grandchild, you are alive! Narin! Nareth! Come here!"

Everyone in the house ran to embrace Chamron and celebrate his return. He was disappointed that his mother and Darab had still not returned.

As much as Chamron wanted to stay with his family, he knew where his responsibilities lay. "I can see you are all doing fine and are taking care of one another," he told them. "I have a responsibility to care for my adopted mother, Ms. Khim, who helped me when I was alone and had no place to go. I left her and her family in Tmorkol Village to come check on you. On my journey here, I heard the Khmer Rouge soldiers launched many rockets and grenades into the college building in Tmorkol Village. Survivors reported that many people were killed, but I was told Ms. Khim escaped to Kadoll Village. I must go and help her move back to Borvel Village. I will return to French Village as soon as possible."

"Go fulfill your promise to Ms. Khim, grandchild. But hurry back to us," Grandma Rang said.

Chamron left his family and reconnected with Ms. Khim in Kadoll Village. They journeyed together to Borvel Village. They stopped in Tmorkol Village overnight and felt safe when they saw North Vietnamese Communist soldiers camping close by. But the soldiers moved during the night, leaving the village unprotected. Chamron's sleep was interrupted by nearby gunfire. He had no idea what was happening, but knew they had to leave right away.

Before daylight, crowds of homeless Cambodians hurried along the highway in the direction of Borvel Village. Later that day, other travelers explained the gunshots to Chamron. These people had narrowly escaped death when the Khmer Rouge soldiers ambushed them in the rice fields. The soldiers hid grenades in the rice grain bundles and watched indifferently as the explosions killed innocent villagers reaching in to get food. Some survivors were captured and forced into slavery by the soldiers.

Chamron's group completed the ten-kilometer journey to Borvel Village. Ms. Khim's relatives welcomed the fatigued travelers. The village had plenty of rice and building supplies, and Ms. Khim's son-in-law and Chamron worked as a team to build a house and barn. After completing the construction projects, Chamron cared for the oxen. He wandered three kilometers with the oxen each day in search of grass. He felt lonely as he sang songs along the way and talked with God. His heart once again was filled with a longing to see his family in French Village.

One day, Chamron received a message Grandma Rang sent through a friend. It read, *My relative in Chomnoum Village has offered to give me twenty bags of rice grain. I need you to borrow Khim's oxen, pick up these bags, and bring them to French Village.*

Chamron ran to Ms. Khim and said, "I have great news! A relative has over two thousand kilograms of rice grain for my family. May I borrow the oxen to transport the heavy load to them?"

Khim's son-in-law, Suhn, spoke first, telling him he could not.

Chamron realized they assumed he would not bring the oxen back to them. No one in the room spoke up to support Chamron and his urgent need to borrow the oxen.

Chamron wondered how they could distrust him. Ms. Khim was clearly different from his real mom, who loved him. Woefully, Chamron realized Ms. Khim would not help him. And there was no way for him to haul the load without the oxen. His family would not get the precious bags of rice grain.

This refusal crushed Chamron's spirit. Brokenhearted, he announced that he would return to his family in French Village. He was stunned when no one objected to his leaving. His stepmom did not ask him to stay. She tossed him a small bit of rice.

Ms. Khim's husband and the neighbors generously gave him more rice and said, "Thank you for caring for our oxen all these months. You've done good work for us."

Without looking back, Chamron hoisted the rice onto his shoulders and headed home. Even the small bag of rice was heavy for him. He was weak, but not bitter. Thoughts of his mother—who genuinely cared for him—brought him comfort. He had been naive to trust Ms. Khim. His heart and spirit were shattered by the realization that her love was a lie.

On his way home, he caught a ride in a wooden cart drawn by oxen to Tmorkol Village. He was blessed with a nap during the ten-kilometer journey.

He awoke when the cart passed through the gate out of Thmorkol Village and jumped off the cart onto a pile of hay by the road. Still drowsy, he lay down and started to close his eyes. But he rolled over when he heard rustling in the bushes.

An old woman moved toward him with a bowl of rice. Without a word, she gave Chamron the rice and disappeared. She was an angel sent by God to provide for him.

Chamron wolfed down the rice and fell asleep.

CHAPTER 14

....

FAMILY REUNITES IN FRENCH VILLAGE

April 1979

Chamron woke up about noon and walked the remaining fifteen kilometers to French Village. His family had no idea he had left Ms. Khim's home. They were astonished to see him approaching their shelter. Everyone rushed forward jubilantly to escort him to the shelter. Chamron was overwhelmed to see his mother among them.

"Mom, I'm so happy that you are alive and here with us!" Chamron exclaimed. "I completed my work at Ms. Khim's home and will not be leaving you again."

His mother, Yorn, replied, "It is wonderful to be here with so many of my children." She looked at each of them. "I've missed you all so much."

Chamron looked around as well. "But, Mother. Where is Darab?"

His mother's face darkened. "I'm sad to tell you that your sister was killed in battle after she was forced to join the Khmer Rouge Communist troops."

Yorn spoke about taking care of orphans in Stung Treng Province near the Laotian border during the war. She loved the fatherless children. Over a bowl of rice porridge, she asked all her children to share stories of what had happened to them during the Khmer Rouge regime.

"My husband, Sai, and I were forced to work in the rice fields in Omany Village," Narin told her. "One day, the Khmer Rouge soldiers dragged Sai from the fields and tortured and killed him. They must have found out that he was the music director in Battambang and taught piano."

"Khmer Rouge leaders tried to force me to marry a stranger," Narith explained to her mother. "I lied and told them I had a fiancé so I could avoid the marriage. I had to do hard labor in the rice fields near Dog Flea Village."

Nareth slowly told his story. "I was sent to a prison camp. A cruel guard kicked me over and over. He hit me in the head with an ax. I have headaches every day. Now I wonder if I can still play the piano and guitar like I used to at church."

"I was taken to a prison camp near Ream Jakrey Village," Nara began. "I reunited with Chamron while working in the rice fields there. I escaped and made it back to Tahen Village where I hid from the soldiers, constantly afraid. I wished every day that Chamron had been able to escape with me."

Prakab shared next. "I'm a fast runner. In Tahen Village, I concealed myself from the Khmer Rouge by rushing around and hiding in bushes. When the soldiers left, I returned to the family shelter. I provided food for the family by killing birds with my slingshot and catching fish."

"Khmer Rouge soldiers took Pratna and me away from Rokar Village to a children's camp," Kosal said. "We were brainwashed to obey Angkar and forced to work in the fields. We were always hungry." He paused, then cried as he continued, "I'll never forget the pain of watching Pratna struggle and die after being given a shot of contaminated liquid from a Coke bottle. Afterward, I escaped and made my way back to Rokar Village, where I had to hide."

Grandma Rang reached out and pulled Sokha to her chest as she said, "Sokha was allowed to stay with me because she was only three years old."

The room was filled with silence and quiet weeping. Chamron folded his hands and bowed his head in prayer before he was able to speak. He shared about his torture and facing near death from disease and starvation. He told them that during his escapes from captivity, he constantly searched for food and places to hide from the Khmer Rouge soldiers. He smiled when he added, "But Jesus was with me and brought me home to you. God is good."

Hearing the unimaginable pain her children had suffered brought tears to Yorn's eyes. As Chamron watched his mother grieve, he remembered the heartbreak of his father dying of cancer. He thought that was the greatest tragedy that could befall the family. Now Chamron knew there was something worse—murder by the Khmer Rouge. His father's passing turned out to be a blessing because as a military officer he would have been tortured and killed by the Khmer Rouge soldiers. Thankfully his father did not live to see the starvation and mass murder of Cambodians.

Chamron paused and thought more about his father. Phallay was a godly man who taught his children the 23rd Psalm. He escorted them to the Catholic church every Sunday and led his family to serve the church and community with volunteer work. Phallay had been a lieutenant in the Cambodian Army and was a respected leader in his community. He played on a championship soccer team for the army and taught his sons soccer skills.

In the funeral procession to the burial site, Chamron had carried a bronze cross, and two of his brothers held large candles. Ten army soldiers marched with them. One soldier waved the Cambodian flag as the others blew trumpets. Phallay's service ended with a twenty-one-gun salute, followed by the presentation of the Cambodian flag to Yorn.

The Khmer Rouge had disrupted all routine family life and instituted laws that prohibited romantic involvement. Groups of fifty people were forced to line up in random order. Whoever was standing in front of you became your spouse. This pairing process continued from 1976 until the end of the Khmer Rouge reign. Narith was fortunate to have escaped the cruel system of forced marriage by telling them she was engaged. In January 1979 when the North Vietnamese Communists took control, most of these married couples separated. There had been no time for romance or passion. The malnourished couples who did get pregnant gave birth to weak babies. Many of these babies died soon after being born.

While Chamron's family was gone, their French Village home was leveled, leaving a pile of rubble. The burned contents were scattered and worthless. Most of the village was vacant and quiet. The shelters were crumbled, crops destroyed, and the livestock was killed. Chamron and his relatives crammed into one of the remaining houses with five other families.

Thirty hungry people glanced around and vowed to care for one another. They searched for ways to feed the crowd. Every week, groups traveled to remote places outside French Village to gather fruits growing wild— coconut, papaya, banana, tamarind, mango, pineapple, and oranges. Vegetables also grew near the forest— morning glories, lettuce, cabbage, broccoli, cauliflower, and turnips. Chickens and pigs ran wild in the streets of the abandoned villages. Everyone shared the little food brought back to the house. A loving spirit filled their hearts.

Every day, Chamron and Prakab gathered wood for cooking fires and hauled water from the Sangker River to keep their seven water jars full. After a full day of hard labor, the two jumped into the Sangker River for a refreshing swim.

Chamron's head rose from the water. He came face to face with the young former Khmer Rouge guard from the sugar cane field. The guard's face turned pale with fear and he scrambled out of the water and dashed away. Chamron had looked into the guard's eyes with compassion, but the man turned away so quickly that he did not see this kind reaction.

Chamron had no desire to seek revenge. He wanted to forgive the young man for wrongly accusing him of stealing sugar cane, but he never saw that man again.

Three months later, most of the trees in the village had been cut down to build shelters and make cooking fires. Consequently, wood was in short supply; parts of the wooden houses had to be burned for cooking. Chamron and Prakab would swim with towing ropes tied around their necks to lasso trees floating in the middle of the Sangker River. The fast-moving water made this difficult, even with the two brothers working together. They would tie rope to a floating log, drag it near the shore, and bind it to a tree. At low tide, the log would lay on the ground, and they could drag it up the muddy bank.

Before cutting the logs into chunks, they'd wait for the sun to dry the mud. Each piece was bulky and heavy. They'd then carry one chunk at a time up a hill by the kitchen room. There, they'd chop the wet wood into smaller pieces, which they then tossed into the field to dry. At the end of the day, the wood was stacked by the kitchen. This process had to be repeated once a week to keep a sufficient wood supply for cooking.

Many Cambodians did not have money. They used rice to barter for clothing and various household items. Chamron's mother managed to set up her food stand in the marketplace beside a few other vendors. She made soup, rice porridge, and noodles. Her business thrived briefly. It ultimately failed, because she had compassion and gave away food to starving beggars. But since she did not get money, she could not buy cooking supplies.

By June 1979, despite everyone's hard work, all food resources had vanished. Chamron's family once again faced starvation.

Nareth left to find a job at the Thailand border. Everyone looked desperately for ways to acquire money and food.

People who knew the Vietnamese language made money translating for the North Vietnamese Communist soldiers who occupied the villages. Some former family friends became hard-hearted and reported misdeeds to the Communists. They were paid to spy on their neighbors. Chamron became suspicious of everyone—never knowing whom he could trust.

In 1970, when Chamron was twelve years old, he had put his trust in his neighbor—a thirty-year-old man. He enjoyed riding to the countryside on the back of this man's bike. The older man got close to Chamron by feeding him good meals at his sister's farm. Once or twice a week for two years, he'd take Chamron under the house and molest him. Chamron, being innocent and still in many ways naïve, did not understand what was happening. All his life, for reasons he could never understand, he kept silent about this abusive treatment.

Chamron's family did not want to leave their beloved Cambodia, but the food shortage made it clear they had no other choice. In July of 1979, Chamron and his mother left French Village with two cups of rice. They headed for the Thai border on a bicycle to look for food. Their plan was to find food and bring it back to the rest of the family. But along the way, the bicycle slipped, and they tumbled onto the hard ground.

As Chamron helped his mother to her feet, he saw blood running down her legs. He held her arms as she hobbled to a relative's house in Svay Sisophorn City. His mother needed to remain there to rest and heal.

Travelers from French Village had arrived at the home the day before. These kind relatives provided rice and salted fish. Chamron joined the group, who were also headed to the Thai border.

Along the way, Chamron became ill, developed a high fever, and could no longer walk. They left him with strangers who allowed him to rest in the shade under their house. Chamron's relatives had to continue without him to reach the border before sundown.

After a few hours, Chamron felt well enough to move on. Night travel was cooler, so he departed in darkness and reached the Thai border at five a.m. He was unable to find his relatives in the throngs jam-packed along the border.

That morning, a group at the border with many bundles hired Chamron to carry their purchases. They marched from the Thai border back to Svay Sisophorn City. He was strong, but had never carried heavy packages for whole days. His shoulders quickly grew sore, but he pushed on with the oppressive load for two days.

For his two days of hard labor, he was paid only fifty milligrams of gold—not even enough to buy one good meal.

CHAPTER 15

....

SELLING GOLD ON THE THAI BORDER

July 1979

Chamron had big plans for the few milligrams of gold he'd received as payment for his arduous work hauling bundles for two days. His mouth watered at the thought of buying moon cakes with egg inside—his favorite treat! He clutched the precious gold and rushed to show it to his brother.

But when he told Nareth his plan, he said, "Do not waste the gold buying cakes. Buy scales and start a business weighing gold."

"What a great idea!" Chamron replied. "I know I can do that and make money."

Chamron rejoined his mom in Svay Sisophorn City and immediately used the gold to buy three Cambodian scales. He carried his new scales as he walked all night to reach the Thai border by four the next morning. He wanted to get the best spot to do his business weighing gold.

When the sun began to rise, he noticed others also weighing gold. One Cambodian man yelled at the Thai people weighing gold, "Those are the wrong scales! You're cheating Cambodian buyers. Your scales are for weighing gemstones not gold. You're cheating us!"

Chamron turned and faced the Cambodian and Thai people on the border. "My scales are handmade in Cambodia. They are balanced correctly to weigh your gold precisely. I'm an honest man who will weigh the gold properly if you pay me."

A man named Kaewta was purchasing gold at the Thai border. This young Thai businessman approached Chamron and asked, "May I buy your handmade scales?"

"No, but I'll weigh your gold accurately if you pay me."

Kaewta smiled kindly. "I think we can work out a business arrangement that will be good for both of us."

Chamron could tell Kaewta trusted him and Chamron soon felt the same about Kaewta. The two men established an agreement which over time grew into a friendship. Each day this deal included rice and small sardine boxes as well as 500 baht for Chamron. Now he was able to support his mom, his relatives, and the three fatherless orphans his family had taken in. He felt God had given him this opportunity to provide for his family. It reminded him of the Old Testament story of Joseph and how God made it possible for him to care for his family during the famine.

Chamron remained at the border working for Kaewta day after day. His brother Prakab carried his earnings and their purchased items to French Village. Chamron was unable to accompany him, because the journey took two days.

Three borderlines were set up between Thailand and Cambodia. The purpose was to protect the Cambodian refugees. The first and second lines were guarded by Cambodian Liberation troops. These soldiers wore camouflage uniforms, and many had long hair. Some of them had been Khmer Rouge soldiers, but they became disillusioned and left after they witnessed the genocide of their people. The troops were fully armed and ready to fight the North Vietnamese Communists. Chamron had planned to join this unit to earn rice for his family. He changed his mind when he witnessed some of the Cambodian Liberation soldiers rob people along the border.

The Pailin Provinces in northwest Cambodia were full of trees and gemstones. Chamron watched miserably as Khmer Rouge soldiers sold his country's precious resources to the Thai. It was also tradition for Cambodian families to invest in gold jewelry, but much of their gold was stolen during this time.

Soldiers continued to ravage the temples and stole statues and sculptures, which they sold to businesspeople in other lands. Other temple contents were thrown into lakes and ponds. Chamron saw them floating, until one by one they sank out of sight. All religion had been methodically eliminated. The monks were still barred from the temples and lived among the people. Their distinctive orange clothing was still black like everyone else's.

The third of the borderlines, the one closest to Thailand, was controlled by Khmer Rouge soldiers. Every morning before daylight, Chamron walked from his shelter along the Thai border and set out his scale by the Khmer Rouge soldiers in Cambodia. Cambodians gathered at the third borderline with their gold to sell for Thai money. They needed Thai money to buy supplies for their loved ones in Cambodia. Chamron enjoyed his dealings with the Cambodian people and gained a reputation for balancing gold fairly.

Each day, Kaewta entrusted Chamron with money to buy gold. He'd hand him a bag with ten kilograms of rice and sardines that hid the Thai money. Chamron would then take the 120,000 baht across the Thai border and buy gold from Cambodians. The gold he purchased consisted of coins, necklaces, earrings, rings, and large pieces of gold. Each transaction took about two hours. While other buyers paid six hundred baht for five ounces of gold, Chamron was a clever man who convinced buyers to sell to him by adding an extra fifty baht to the deal.

During the routine business of purchasing gold for Kaewta, Chamron noticed the large displays of gold jewelry for sale. He never considered buying jewelry for his family; his entire focus was on working fast and buying for Kaewta. The gold-buying business was dangerous because of the large sums of money involved. Chamron never worried about his safety though. He could have been killed or robbed at any time, but he felt confident that God protected him.

Two of Chamron's friends, Seoung and Soun, assisted him in this business. Seoung hid in a tree and whistled if he saw thieves coming. Soun weighed the gold while Chamron handled the money. He paid his friends well for their help. After spending all Kaewta's money, he'd deliver the gold to him in the Thai village. Kaewta spoke a few Cambodian words and Chamron knew enough Thai to carry on business. The partnership was profitable for both men.

Each morning at five, Chamron and his two friends traveled through the three borderlines. The darkness made it hard to tell if the gold was real. Kaewta warned him that some of the gold he had bought for him had silver inside. Chamron never wanted to be cheated again, so he did some research and developed three ways to test the gold:

- He carried a bottle of acid in his backpack. A drop of acid on gold has no effect, but a fake will burn.
- Real gold will not scratch when rubbed on a rock, but fakes will be covered with marks.

- A candle held up to the gold will not burn it, but fakes burst into flame.
- He bought a small saw. Sometimes he had to cut the large gold pieces to assure no silver was inside.

Kaewta was a single man who lived with his mother and brother. Once in a while, Kaewta took Chamron to his house. While Kaewta sold the gold in Bangkok, Chamron waited at the house and visited with Kaewta's mother. In the late afternoon, when Kaewta would return, he'd give Chamron a bag of money covered with rice and sardines. Chamron would carefully hide the bag in his towel he wore around his waist, then join the family for an evening meal.

One time, Kaewta invited Chamron to go with him to see a movie. But it was illegal for a Cambodian to be in Thailand at night without a passport, and they knew that discovery would lead to a beating by Thai soldiers and possible imprisonment. So Kaewta set about disguising his young friend. He first dressed Chamron in a brightly colored shirt and pants, a style vastly different from the all-black clothing Cambodians still wore. He further disguised him with a big hat to cover his face, because Thai and Cambodian facial features are so different.

After the movie, Chamron showered and slept comfortably on a mat in the main room of Kaewta's home. The next morning, Chamron hopped behind

Kaewta on a motorcycle and they headed to the border. Being aware of the dangers they might face, Kaewta carried a gun for protection. He waited near the border while Chamron conducted the gold business in Cambodia. They had a set time and place to meet when he was finished.

After two months of working for Kaewta, Chamron made enough money to move his family from Svay Sisophorn City to New Camp, which was near the border. He wanted Kaewta and his brother to meet his family. He planned a party and prepared a buffet of his favorite foods.

The day of their visit, some Cambodian Liberation soldiers at the border insisted on joining the party. The soldiers devoured the food and drank themselves into a drunken state as they celebrated with Chamron and his friends. In his enthusiasm, one of the Cambodian soldiers hugged Kaewta and felt his gun. He jerked back in anger and pointed his weapon at Kaewta yelling, "Why are you hiding a gun?"

Kaewta stiffened and glared at the man. Everyone was suddenly very tense. He told the soldiers, "I carry this gun for protection when I travel."

Chamron stepped between the soldier and Kaewta. "Stop! Put your gun down. Kaewta is a good man."

The soldier lowered his gun and listened.

Chamron continued, "We have a business relationship and have become friends. I brought him here to meet my family. He is not the enemy."

The soldier regained his composure and walked out.

When the soldiers were gone, Kaewta embraced Chamron. "I could have been shot. Thank you for stepping in."

Before any further conflict, Chamron led his friends back to the Thai border. Over the next months, they worked together and developed an even more trusting friendship.

Despite the dangers, people traveled back and forth along the border doing business. When Chamron was not working, he lived in New Camp near the soldiers. The Cambodian Liberation Army commanders along the border changed sometimes, and it was important to Chamron's safety to make friends with the new chiefs and commanders. He made it a point to be sociable and take cigarettes, wine, and beer to the guards. Sometimes he invited them to share a meal with him.

Chamron had to pass through all three borderlines to buy gold. Three Cambodian soldiers, who were always working near Chamron, also bought gold. One day after work, Chamron and his friends spotted a passport photo on the path in the rice field. The photo was of one of three soldiers that Chamron saw every day.

Chamron pointed to the picture. "Soun, would you please pick up that picture for me?"

"Why would I want an ugly picture of a dark-skinned man?" Soun asked. "Too bad it is not a beautiful woman."

Chamron felt a mental nudge from the Lord. Without saying a word, he picked up the photo and put it in his pocket.

The next day started out in a routine way. Chamron had 120,000 baht safely hidden in the towel around his waist. The three friends walked from the first border to the second. They were about to reach the third borderline when Chamron noticed three soldiers armed with rifles. He recognized them as the three soldiers who also bought gold near where he typically set up. One of them was the man whose passport photo he still held. As they moved cautiously past the soldiers, Chamron heard a warning from the Lord: *Be prepared. They're going to try to rob you.*

Chamron sat down when he heard the warning. He lay out his towel, set up his scale, and started buying gold on the spot. In a short time, he'd spent 10,000 baht buying a little gold.

From up in a tree, Seoung whistled a warning. Chamron glanced up from his work and recognized the three gunmen moving in his direction. He knew that when they saw him, they would recognize him as the buyer who paid extra for the gold to get more business.

Chamron hastily wrapped the scales, money, and gold in his towel and threw it a few yards away. He shoved Soun out of sight.

Chamron prayed, "Save me, Jesus," then the peace of the Lord settled over him and kept him from freezing in fear. He did not panic or beg for mercy. He reminded himself that God had given him this profitable job. He remained confident that He would protect him and this money for his family.

The men surrounded him and waved their guns in a menacing manner. Glaring at Chamron, they demanded he answer their questions. In rapid succession, one soldier yelled, "Where's the money? Where're your scales? Show me the money or we'll blow your head off."

Chamron stood up and said, "I have nothing." He held his arms up in the air and said, "Come here. Inspect my body."

The soldiers paced around Chamron looking for the money. They never saw the towel lying in plain sight a few feet away. Chamron was sure God blinded their eyes to protect him.

In frustration, the soldiers struck Chamron with their guns. He collapsed to the ground and moaned as they punched him over and over. When the beating was over, he reared up on his elbows and finally stood.

The soldiers walked a short distance away, then opened fire with their AK-47s. Chamron flinched at the sound and wrapped his arms around his body. Closing his eyes, he prayed, "God, if I die, take me to heaven."

Bullets continued to spray over his head. For a few long minutes, he kept his eyes tightly shut. He waited once it was silent, then gradually glanced around. He frantically touched parts of his body, checking for wounds. Nothing but dust coated him.

A soldier rushed over, struck him again, and yelled, "Start walking!"

With a gun poking his back, Chamron staggered forward. The soldiers screamed at the people watching, "This man is a traitor!" They marched to the third borderline, where Chamron recognized some Khmer Rouge guards that were his friends. These guards could have killed his captors. God told Chamron not to allow them to interfere. He signaled his friends to step aside. Fortunately, the tired soldiers wanted nothing more to do with Chamron and released him at the border.

As soon as the gunmen left with Chamron, Seoung and Soun had broken into action. They'd grabbed the towel and delivered the money to Kaewta. They cried as they reported Chamron's capture. Everyone assumed he had been killed.

Though the gunmen had left Chamron at the border, he understood he was not out of harm's way. He recalled the passport photo in his pocket. He handed the photo to the chief commander at the border and said, "Three men tried to rob me. This is a photo of one of the men. They beat me with their guns and shot at me. They intend to kill me and my family."

This news enraged the chief commander. He yelled at his soldiers, "Find these three men and put them in jail for twenty-four hours." Their brief imprisonment gave Chamron time to protect his family by evacuating them to Kok Kyoong Village—about five kilometers from New Camp.

The next morning, Chamron strolled through the marketplace with his friend, whose father was commander of Kok Kyoong Village. He gasped when he spied the three gunmen approaching with seven other men. They had followed him.

The large rockets and high-powered rifles on their shoulders made it clear they planned to kill him. These ten heavily armed men thrust Chamron into the middle of their group. They shoved his friend aside and focused their scowling eyes on Chamron.

Nosey onlookers encircled them. The three gunmen jabbed Chamron with their guns and shouted, "Kill him. Don't let him go. He accused us of robbery." The three men kicked and viciously beat him.

Chamron curled up on the ground and prayed, "Save me, Jesus. I have only You in my life. My Savior, Protector, Redeemer."

Chamron heard the voice of his friend's father, the chief commander of Kok Kyoong Village, "What's happening? Why're you blocking the marketplace?"

The curious onlookers stepped aside. The commander forced the gunmen to move away. Grabbing Chamron by the arm, he said, "Son, let's go and have a drink." They marched off together.

Silently, the ten gunmen watched them walk away. Intimidated by the rank of this high commander, they scattered and never bothered Chamron again. His friend's father had rescued him from certain death. God had used him to save Chamron.

Every time he cried out to Jesus, Chamron was saved.

CHAPTER 16

....

LIFE IN THAI REFUGEE CAMPS

November 1979

With the ten gunmen from the Kok Kyoong marketplace no longer following him, Chamron resumed his business of selling gold for Kaewta. While working along the Thai border, he again spotted the soldier from the passport photo patrolling the area. When he saw Chamron, he turned and hurried away.

Chamron had no wish to seek revenge on this man who had beaten and tortured him. Instead, he felt compassion for the frightened man. Chamron went about his business, and he never saw the man again.

Passing over the border from Cambodia into Thailand was illegal without a passport—which no Cambodians had. Still, Cambodian refugees risked their lives by crossing over the Thai border to buy food and supplies to sell in Cambodia. Thai soldiers did not want the Cambodians to do business in their land. There was the constant possibility of robbery or, even worse, death. Thai robbers, gunmen, and soldiers attacked the Cambodians. Women traveling alone were beaten, raped, and had no protection once they entered the country. These assaults on the refugees created tension, bitterness, resentment, and conflict between the Cambodian Liberation soldiers and the Thai soldiers.

An additional hazard was the ten million landmines scattered in Cambodia. The Khmer Rouge Army laid the land mines, but they never mapped them. Since the time of the Killing Fields, many Cambodians have lost their lives or limbs when they step on a hidden mine. Today there are warning signs painted with skull and crossbones that read, *Danger! Mines!* For years trained people have been removing the active land mines, but millions still remain.

Early one morning, Chamron, Nareth, Nara, and Prakab were awakened in Kok Kyoong Village by the sound of gunfire. Bullets whizzed by their heads. Thai soldiers were launching rockets into the refugee camp. The family ducked and felt the flurry of dust and debris on their legs as rockets landed nearby. Chamron and his brothers ran and jumped into some bushes under a hill and huddled together for protection and support.

Sirens alerted people to take shelter. Patrolling airplanes hovered close to the ground. In the midst of the noisy assault, the brothers yelled to one another.

Prakab, the youngest, held on to Chamron. "Stay close to me!" he cried.

Chamron hugged him tightly. "Just stay down low!"

They looked up and saw many Buddhist followers gathered on the top of the same hill. The head monk assembled the frightened people and chanted loudly for protection. Chamron watched the monks grab the large beads around their necks and touch them as they chanted. People became silent and listened. Tears streamed down their faces, and they shook with fear. None of the rockets near Chamron ever exploded; however, he witnessed explosions all around the area.

From their hiding place in the bushes, the brothers saw many people in need of help. One rocket hit an outhouse. The man inside screamed. The brothers rushed to help him. They lifted him from the debris and saw that half of his bottom was gone. He was unconscious and bleeding. They rushed him to a small makeshift nursing station. Leaving him there, they hurried off to help others lying on the ground, unable to move. Chamron and his brothers carried the injured people to an area near the border to receive care. Numerous Cambodians were wounded or killed that day. After this attack, Chamron's family moved five kilometers west to another camp called Nong Chan. Their stay in this Cambodian refugee camp along the border was brief.

Chamron watched as many Cambodians boarded United Nation buses that had come to rescue them. The buses went to Khao I Dang refugee camp in Thailand. On November 22, 1979, Chamron gathered his mom, Grandma Rang, and his siblings—Narin, Narith,

Nareth, Nara, Prakab, Kosal, and Sokha. He escorted them to one of the United Nations buses. His family filled that bus, so Chamron boarded the next bus. He knew it was his last day in his homeland. He loved Cambodia and wished to stay, but it was too risky. He hoped one day to return to a free Cambodia.

As soon as the buses entered the gates of the camp, the refugees off-loaded and lined up to proceed through a checkpoint staffed with nurses and doctors. Tent clinics were set up to treat the weak and wounded. Each person was given a cup of water and a few pills. Many refugees needed medical care.

Chamron reunited with his family in Khao I Dang, the largest refugee camp in Thailand—thirteen kilometers from Nong Chan Camp. There were 130,000 refugees crowded into two square kilometers of land. People in the camps were divided into groups and given food, clean water, mats, pillows, blankets, and mosquito netting. The days were hot, but at sundown the air became cold. Bamboo, nails, wire, and palm leaves were provided for building shelters. Families were expected to cook their own meals using rice and vegetables distributed to them. They gathered firewood in the mountain forests. They had buckets for drawing water from a central water tank.

Some Khmer Rouge refugees came to Khao I Dang camp in a bus from Srahker refugee camp in Thailand. When Cambodian refugees saw them, they ran to the bus and recognized the Khmer Rouge who had tortured and killed their families. The angry group took revenge and immediately killed many of them.

Chamron never dreamed he would be in refugee camps for two and a half years—from November 23, 1979 until March 8, 1982. He was leader of Unit Nineteen, which was near the soccer field. Every week, he gathered supplies from the central area and delivered them to the families. Chamron's future wife, Lekun Chhom, and her family—the Noeums—were in his group. From the day he entered this camp, Lekun's immediate family and her cousins witnessed to Chamron. Up to this point in his travels, he had never met any followers of Jesus. Each day, he continued to pray, "Save me, Jesus." He also recited the Lord's Prayer that he learned as a child from his father. But when Lekun's family encouraged him to attend evening Bible study with them, he was filled with pride and a bit of arrogance, so he refused to participate. His focus in the refugee camps was on day-to-day survival and he fully expected to hear soon that Cambodia was once again peaceful and that he could go home. He had forgotten about the covenant he had made with God in the Killing Fields when he cried, "Save me, Jesus! I promise to serve You the rest of my life."

In December of 1979, Lekun's siblings came to Chamron with a fresh approach. While Chamron lay in a hammock, whistling and singing to himself, they led a group of children to him. The children stood in front of him and burst into song:

Years I spent in vanity and pride,
Caring not my Lord was crucified,
Knowing not it was for me he died
On Calvary.

Mercy there was great, and grace was free;
Pardon there was multiplied to me;
There my burdened soul found liberty
at Calvary.

By God's Word at last my sin I learned;
Then I trembled at the law I'd spurned,
Till my guilty soul imploring turned
To Calvary.

Now I've giv'n to Jesus everything,
Now I gladly own him as my King,
Now my raptured soul can only sing
Of Calvary!

Oh, the love that drew salvation's plan!
Oh, the grace that brought it down to man!
Oh, the mighty gulf that God did span
At Calvary![1]

After hearing the fourth stanza, Chamron jumped off the hammock, fell to his knees, and opened his heart. He humbly prayed, "Lord Jesus, I am a sinner. Please forgive my sins. I receive You as my Lord and Savior."

---

[1] "At Calvary"; William R. Newell/Daniel B. Towner; 1895

In that moment, he realized he was a child of God. His transformation had begun, and he was filled with a desire to follow God and serve Him.

In the Killing Fields, he'd asked to be saved from physical death. Now, at the age of twenty-two, he experienced spiritual salvation.

And at last, he knew he was truly saved.

CHAPTER 17

....

NEW LIFE IN A NEW LAND

January 1980

Forty thousand Cambodian refugees became Christians during this time. Chamron calls this time "The Great Awakening," because never before had so many Cambodians become followers of Jesus. Chamron received a New Testament during a Gideon distribution of Bibles. For the first time, he began studying the Bible.

Every day, he spent personal time with God as he read. He attended morning prayers led by Cambodian pastors, he joined several of the small Bible study groups, and he enrolled in Bible training led by missionaries and pastors. He eagerly searched for every opportunity to learn more and more about Jesus. He had a thirst for biblical knowledge and a desire to grow spiritually.

While believers grew rapidly in numbers, problems also increased. Some allegiances focused on individual church leaders, rather than on Jesus. A rumor was spread throughout the camp by non-believers that

Christians would be sent back to Cambodia, where they would face persecution. In fear, some threw away their Bibles and quit going to church, while Christian leaders worked to stop the spread of false stories and bring the people back to the church.

Chamron's personal faith grew as he walked with God and spent time in the Word. Lekun and her family attended the Protestant Church services in Khao I Dang camp. Lekun's cousin saw Chamron's enthusiasm for God's Word and showed him a Bible with both the Old and New Testaments. She told him to visit Pastor Sokung Nehm and recite scriptures for him. If he did this, he would be given a complete Bible. Chamron went to see Pastor Nehm right away and got his own Bible.

One day, Lekun's mother, Yokra, turned to Chamron and asked, "Would you be willing to teach children the Word of God?"

Chamron paused and asked for time to pray about her request. During his prayer time, he realized God was using Yokra as an instrument to call him to lead a children's ministry.

After a few days, he answered Yokra. "The Lord has put it on my heart to teach the children about Jesus."

Every evening, he sat with children outside under a tree. He told Bible stories and led singing with his guitar. For ten months, he faithfully spent time with the children.

The Word of God was being spread through the work of Christian missionaries from Canada, England, Switzerland, France, and the United States. Several Christian organizations worked in the camps:

- Overseas Missionary Fellowship (OMF)
- Christian Missionary Alliance (CMA)
- Campus Crusade for Christ (CCC)
- Youth With a Mission (YWAM)
- Gideons International
- Catholic priests and missionaries

Catholic priests met weekly with groups of refugees in the camps. They faithfully ministered to the physical and spiritual needs of the Catholic believers. Worship services were held each week.

Chamron learned English by studying the Bible with people from the various Christian organizations. Every Sunday, many refugees attended the Protestant Church in Khao I Dong camp. They had used bamboo, hay, and palm leaves to build a church that seated 1500 on benches. An additional 500 gathered outside to listen to the Word of God. Each week, many walked up the stairs of the nearby water tank to be baptized. Six months after declaring himself to be a follower of Jesus, Chamron made the climb up the steps to be baptized.

There were 40,000 Christians in this refugee camp. They started each day with prayer in the main church building. This was followed by further worship in the fifty small church structures constructed throughout the camp. Daily groups of fifteen to sixty people studied God's Word together.

During his journey of faith in Christ, Chamron had three Cambodian pastors help him grow in grace and knowledge of the Word. Om Ong was an elderly pastor with a peaceful demeanor. Each day, he showed Chamron the truths in the Bible. Chamron read through the Old Testament four times. Pastor Chan Lim and Pastor Rouy Yun took time to answer Chamron's many questions about God. Time with these pastors instilled in Chamron a strong desire to seek seminary training.

Eventually, all the pastors were transferred to different refugee camps. Before leaving, these pastors met and prayed about the ministry in Khao I Dang camp. They unanimously decided to ask Chamron to take on the responsibility of leading the adult Bible studies, youth ministry, and evangelistic outreach.

Pastor Chan Lim represented the three pastors. He came to Chamron and explained, "Chamron, we have been transferred to other camps and will be leaving soon. God has led us to you as the one to take over leadership of our Bible studies in this camp. Go now, and prayerfully consider doing this work."

Chamron walked away and went into prayer. After three days, Chamron walked back to Pastor Chan Lim's shelter. "After praying, I feel God is calling me to serve Him in these ministries. I'll lead youth ministry and do evangelism during the day. I'm a new believer, but I'll do my best to lead the adult Bible study in the evenings."

Because of his long hair, Chamron was sometimes accused of being a gangster and robber. At that time, people with long hair would sneak into the camp at night with guns and knives and steal. Long-haired people became targets, accused of robbery. He and his brother-in-law were the only ones who lived in their camp with long hair.

One day, on a trip to the marketplace to buy ice cream, Chamron wore a sarong. A Thai soldier stared at him, looking him up and down.

Chamron did not turn around; he tried to remain calm as he prayed, "Save me, Lord Jesus."

Apparently deciding he was not a threat, the soldier yelled, "Keep moving, woman."

That frightening experience convinced Chamron to cut his hair much shorter.

In 1980, Mr. Brown from the United Nations held a meeting to discuss sponsorship. There were two options:

- Apply to go to any country in the world
- Apply to go back to Cambodia (Buses waited to take people across the Thai border.)

At this 1980 meeting, Chamron and his family members applied for sponsorship to America. It took two years for them to get final approval.

Lekun Chhom's family of ten received sponsorship from an auntie, and relocated to Oakland, California in 1980. Before they left, Chamron exchanged photos with Lekun.

Lekun and her family spent a year in Manila, Philippines before making it to Oakland. During this time, Chamron and Lekun exchanged letters, eventually making plans to marry. They trusted God to bring them back together.

Chamron, his mother, Grandma Rang, Narin, Prakab, Kosal, and Sokha were moved to Chonbury Camp. There, Chamron played his guitar and led songs of praise to Jesus each Sunday. He met Rosa Brand, a missionary from OMF in Switzerland, who gave him a set of panoramic Bible story pictures. Chamron showed the inspirational pictures to Grandma Pok, a friend he'd made in Khao I Dang camp. They decided to partner and use the pictures to evangelize in Chonbury Camp and in other nearby refugee camps.

A special pass was needed to travel between the camps. These passes were difficult to obtain. Chamron and his friend Grandma Pok approached the gate one day without a pass.

Chamron whispered to Grandma Pok. "Pray for me."

Grandma Pok prayed, "God, if You want us to go to the other camps, open the door for us according to Your will."

They arrived at the gate and the Thai soldier saw they did not have a pass. He asked, "What're you doing? Why do you want to go into this camp?"

Chamron held up a Bible picture. Grandma Pok gathered her courage and said, "We want to share this story with the people in the camps."

After that day, the Thai soldier let them go to the camps any time without a pass. God had worked another miracle.

In the fall of 1981, Chamron's family's name appeared on the list to go to America. All seven of them were interviewed by Immigration and Naturalization Service and given physical exams. They sighed with relief when they all passed, and an officer stamped their documentation: *Approved!*

Having successfully gone through that process, they received authorization to move to Lum Phiny Camp in Bangkok. During their six months in this camp, Chamron led Bible studies and translated some of the Christian curriculum into Cambodian for the missionaries. On Sundays, he preached to about forty people who gathered to worship.

Before leaving Thailand, each person had to sign a contract with the airlines promising to pay them back once they got jobs. The cost was $500 per person. Upon reaching America, they each faithfully made payments every month. It would take them several years to pay off the debt.

On March 9, 1982, Chamron's family flew on a Pan Am plane to San Francisco, California. He carried a black garbage bag with his one set of extra clothing, a pair of shoes, a Bible, and some Christian song books.

He had given his guitar to the church at the Lum Phiny Camp.

As soon as he stepped off the plane, he gave thanks and praise to God for bringing him to this land of freedom.

Chamron wondered what plans God had for him. His family was bused to temporary housing at Hamilton Air Force Base in San Francisco, where they stayed for a week. He immediately wanted to contact Lekun and her family, but no one was allowed to make phone calls. During that week, Chamron's family learned they had received sponsorship from the International Institute Association in Boston, and that was where they had to go.

After a week, Chamron's family flew to Boston, Massachusetts. That day, a huge blizzard buried the city in snow. None of them had ever seen snow. They looked around in amazement and shivered in their thin clothing. Like little children, they reached out their hands to catch snowflakes. This strange new place appeared to be a fairy land, blanketed in white. Before they had time to catch their breath and figure out the phenomenon called snow, representatives from the International Institute hurried them off in two separate cars. A translator gave them a little money and took them to a furnished apartment in Allston, Massachusetts, near Cambridge.

The apartment had a heater, a TV, kitchen utensils for each person, blankets, pillows, and foam mats. They were especially thankful for the heater.

Two feet of snow fell that night. Without proper clothing, Chamron and his sister walked in the snow to a market to buy fruit, milk, and water bottles. They did not realize the tap water was safe to drink. Their mother washed their clothes in the bathtub and hung them outside to dry. Then they crawled onto the foam mats at about four a.m. and fell asleep. They were exhausted.

In the morning, they were surprised to find the clothes they'd hung outside were now frozen solid. They had begun to realize just how unfamiliar this place was. Still, words could not contain their gratefulness to have made it this far.

Chamron looked out the window and stared into a strange new world. He imagined Grandpa Nguon there, listening to his radio, smiling at him. Seven years ago, before their lives became a nightmare, his family had all been together, preparing to celebrate the New Year. Now, what was left of them prepared to begin their new lives in a new place—a place none of them knew.

Chamron had lost so much since that day in 1975. He had suffered immeasurably and had lived for years in fear of what was to come. But on this day, God spoke these reassuring words to him:

There is no more enemy. The tiger is gone.

Made in the USA
San Bernardino, CA
09 July 2020

75182955R00119